Through The Portal

Pleiadian Perspective on Ascension

Book 5

Suzanne Lie, Ph.D.

CONTENTS

Pleiadian Perspective on Ascension Book 5
Through The Portal

CHANGING REALITIES
Part 1 ~ Another Trip to the Airport
Part 2 ~ A Wonderful Reunion
Part 3 ~ The Arcturian's Message
Part 4 ~ Gaia's Message

LEMURIAN LEADERSHIP
Part 1 ~ Sanat Kumara Speaks
Part 2 ~ A Morning Message
Part 3 ~ Communicating with All Life
Part 4 ~ Asking For Guidance

BACK FROM LEMURIA
Part 1 ~ Our New Life
Part 2 ~ Arcturian Campsite Message
Part 3 ~ Communicating with Ether and Earth
Part 4 ~ Communicating With Sylphs and Undines

TRANSMUTATION OF LIFE
Part 1 ~ Living In-Between
Part 2 ~ Kundalini, the Inner Fire

Suzanne Lie, Ph.D.

Part 3 ~ Adapting To The Shift
Part 4 ~ The Beginning
Part 5 ~ Transmuting the Core Crystal

Afterward
How It All Began

About the Author

Other Books from the Author

Through The Portal

Suzanne Lie, Ph.D.

CHANGING REALITIES

Suzanne Lie, Ph.D.

Changing Realities Part 1

Another Trip to the Airport

JASON SPEAKS:

I woke up with a start to find Sandy just awakening next to me.

"WOW, I had an amazing dream," I said as soon as Sandy opened her eyes.

"Yes me too! But, I am thinking that it was NOT a dream," Sandy said in her groggy morning voice.

"Yes," I replied. "Do you think we were on another journey?"

"I am not sure. Let me get us some coffee and we can swap dreams. In fact, maybe we should write them down while we drink our coffee and then share them. If we come up with the same or very similar dreams, we will know we were on another adventure."

"Great idea," I said as I pulled myself from the bed in search of something to wear.

When Sandy came in with my coffee I was dressed and fully awake. "Let's go sit at the kitchen table and write while we sip our coffee."

"Yes, you go ahead. I am going to get dressed too. Then I will get my coffee and join you."

Through The Portal

We wrote our dreams by hand as it was too cumbersome to type and drink coffee, and neither one of us wanted to surrender our coffee. When I began to write, I realized that I had no sense of time. I had to get my phone to check the date and time. Was it really one day later? It seemed like so much had happened, but I could not remember what.

The last thing I could remember was Sandy and I going outside to check for Starships. No, then I remembered our friends coming over, but was that a different day? I could see from Sandy's face that she was as confused as I was. We had decided to not talk until we had written our story, but I was not sure what to write.

It seemed like many different things were all happening at the same time, and my human brain was struggling to put these events into some form of timeline. Finally, I gave up and just wrote the events as they came into my memory. However, there is no way that all those things could have happened in one night. We must have lost a lot of time.

I checked the calendar again to see that, yes, only one night had passed. I was just thinking that it was if we had left time when Sandy said, "I am so confused. There is no way that all of this could have happened in one day!"

We laughed together when we realized that we had both had the same idea. We knew that the Arcturian had talked quite a bit about living in the no-time of the NOW, but we thought that could only happen on the Ship. However, we were right here on planet Earth, at least until…

"Mytrian was with us," shouted Sandy in excitement.

"There is only NOW," we both said laughingly as we began to remember.

Sandy got up to get us some more coffee. When she returned we drank the coffee and shared our notes. It was very interesting to see how we experienced the same events from our own personal experience. Sandy remembered more of the feelings and communications, whereas I remembered more of the details and the sequence of events.

"Together, we created a pretty precise account of our experience," I said as I shook Sandy's hand. But, she was not as excited.

"No," she said. "There is something more. Something that we have not done yet, but we promised we would do."

"Can we take a day off first?" I said in a teasing manner, but I did mean it. I was exhausted and needed to rest and recreate before I took on the next assignment. Hmm, I thought, it was an assignment.

"It seems that we volunteered to do," said Sandy, again responding to my thoughts. "But I agree, I need some 'NOW' to relax and regroup. Can we go to the meadow and have a picnic?"

"I am on it," I said. "You take a shower first and I will make the sandwiches."

Before I finished my sentence, Sandy was off to the shower. I knew I would have some time to make the food as Sandy looked like she needed a long shower.

It turned out that I, too, needed a long shower. Hence, it was almost lunchtime before we got to the meadow. It was a beautiful day, so after we ate, we lied on the blanket, relaxed and catnapped. We stayed there most of the day, and only the cool breeze before sunset made us pack up the car to go home.

We were not ready to go home and decided to go by the airport to see what version of reality we would find. We had not turned on the news, opened our computers or read a newspaper, so we had no idea if we were the only ones to have our experience. However, we had finally gone beyond doubt, especially since we each wrote the same events from our own different perspectives.

As we drove down the hill toward the airport, we could feel our expectations fill the car. We had no idea what we would find, as the airport seemed to be some kind of vortex in which time slipped back and forth into what we would call the future or the past.

We knew that there is only NOW and that both future and past are illusions. On the other hand, while we were in our physical selves, we had to fight thinking that our higher dimensional experiences were the illusion. How long would it take for us to resolve this paradox? OOPS, that is thinking in 3D time again.

One thing that Sandy and I did figure out while we were relaxing, dozing and talking in the meadow was that when we thought in terms of "time," we experienced only the physical world.

On the other hand, when we thought in terms of "NOW," we began to experience our multidimensional world. Since we had spent the day lounging in the NOW of the meadow, perhaps we could experience the higher dimensional airport.

"I hope we get to see the future, galactic airport instead of the beat up one that we have now," said Sandy. She had also slipped into thinking in terms of time. Just ahead was a turnout and I pulled the car into it. We could not see the airport form this location, but it would soon come into view.

"Sandy," I said before she could ask why I had pulled the car over. "We are both thinking in time again. We know that if we think in time we only see the third dimension."

"Yes, yes, you are right," she exclaimed. "Did you park here so that we can return to the NOW we had in the meadow?"

"You read my mind again dear," I replied. "Let's meditate for a bit so that we can focus on the NOW. Also, it appears that Mytrian is a big part of all this. Perhaps we should both focus on Mytrian."

"Yes, that would give us a joint focus. How should we start?" asked Sandy.

"Is that really Mytrian sitting on the front of our car, or is that just an illusion?" I said.

"All the physical world is an illusion," Mytrian said as he levitated just above the car. (At some point in the NOW, Sandy and I had decided to call Mytrian "he," as "he/she" was too cumbersome and "it" was too impersonal.)

While Sandy and I focused on Mytrian floating before us, we gradually went into a very deep meditation. At first all we saw was a void, and then gradually a Starship came into our awareness. The interesting thing is that we both knew we were experiencing exactly the same thing.

"Which reality do you choose to perceive?" we heard Mytrian speaking with the usual lilt he had in his voice. Our eyes flew open. We looked at each other and simultaneously said, "I choose a galactic reality."

Without a word, I started the engine, turned onto the road, and drove around the curve towards the airport. Before I rounded the second curve, Sandy and I heard Mytrian telepathically say, "Everything that expresses itself fits into the overall picture that creates the conditions and events that are experienced by everyone."

Since the road was quite steep and curving in this section of the road, I had to focus on driving and allow Mytrian's words to sink into my consciousness. However, I could feel that Sandy was having an extreme reaction to Mytrian's statement, so I went into the next turnout of the road to talk to her.

"Sandy," I said with a concerned voice. "Are you OK?"

All she could do was shake her head "NO" while she waved me to continue to the bottom of the mountain where the road became flat and straight. I decided to trust her and pulled out of the turnout to carefully drive down to the highway where I pulled to the nearby rest area. Sandy had closed her eyes and gone into a meditative state, likely to contain the energy she was feeling.

"Please talk to me now," I said. "I am at the bottom of the hill in the rest area."

Slowly she opened her eyes and looked at me. "I didn't want to say anything as you had to drive us down the hill. But, when Mytrian made his last statement I was suddenly engulfed, and still am, with myriad possible realities all occurring at the same NOW. I knew if I told you, you would have the same experience and not be able to drive."

With her last words, I began to share her experience. I was seeing multiple possible realities all at once. Sandy was correct. I could not have driven down the hill in this condition. I could feel us both becoming increasingly dizzy when Sandy said, "We have to focus on the same reality."

"But which one?" I replied. "There are so many all at once and intermingled with each other."

"What reality do you want to see?" Mytrian asked.

"We want to see the galactic reality of New Earth," I said knowing Sandy would agree.

I could feel our joint consciousness searching through all the moving pictures in our minds to find a reality in which the Earth had become a galactic society. Since Sandy found that reality first, she verbally explained it to me so that I could join her. Finally, the myriad moving pictures congealed into one picture of the modern version of the airport building.

We both focused on the Starships "parked" high above us, the scout ships parked below them and closer to earth and the shuttlecraft landed and landing on the ground. Sandy explained how all the people were very calm about this experience as they were totally accustomed to this reality.

"Yes, yes," I proclaimed. "I can see it all now. The people are very relaxed even though there are Galactics that are not humanoids. I am going to open my eyes now. I think I am ready to drive."

"I will continue to tell you about this version of reality so we can stay in synch until we reach the airport."

Through The Portal

I shook my head yes and continued to focus on her words as I drove to the airport.

Changing Realities Part 2

A Wonderful Reunion

JASON SPEAKS:

We arrived at the airport about an hour before sunset. The light was a bit dim, but we could still clearly see that we had indeed arrived at the modern airport. The building was completely transformed from the old fashioned one that we had once seen and now had sleek lines and large windows.

Most importantly, the sky was filled with Starships. The larger ones were "parked" high in the sky, the smaller ones closer to the earth, and there were several very large ships that were so high that they were distant shadows. There were also scout ships close by or landed in the airport. In the east, I saw something that looked exactly like Sandy's image.

I wondered if maybe the dim light was playing tricks on my vision until a large scout ship buzzed over us and landed close by. Instantly, two tall blond beings in blue uniforms exited the ship and walked swiftly towards us.

Even though the light was dim, Sandy and I could quickly identify them as Mytre and

Mytria. We started to walk towards them, and then Sandy began to run. She ran to Mytria and hugged her. Mytria warmly returned her hug. Sandy then hugged Mytre, while I continued to walk towards them not sure if I could maintain my *masculine aloofness*.

"Oh, come on Jason," said Sandy with a big smile. "You know you want to hug them too."

Mytria made it easy for me by stepping forward to greet me with a big hug. Even Mytre hugged me saying that Pleiadian men were very openly affectionate. In fact, he asked me why I did not remember that fact. Was he telling me that I was a Pleiadian?

"Of course he is telling you that," said Sandy responding to my thoughts again. "I guess that makes me a Pleiadian too. How cool is that?"

To our surprise and great joy Mytre and Mytria directed us to their scout ship so that we could go inside. I was taken aback when Mytre directed me to sit at the helm and began instructing - actually he used the words 'reminding'- me how to pilot this ship. I was even more astounded when I suddenly remembered just what to do.

Sandy was beaming with pride for me, but stayed away to not interfere with my moment. Mytre then stepped in between us and started *reminding* me about the navigation and communication systems. I felt myself slipping into the NOW. Once I had totally released time, my mind burst forth with memories of my true life as a Pleiadian member of the Arcturian Starship Athena.

I had the amazing experience of perceiving myself in a multidimensional fashion. I was in the scout ship wearing a human vessel, on the Starship as my Pleiadian self, and recognized my self as a distinguished member of the Galactic Federation. I also had a strong sense of my human child self when I almost died while swimming in the nearby lake.

Suddenly, I was only the child on the verge of drowning. The surface of the water was far above me, but I did not care. I was experiencing a wonderful moment of total peace and calmness. Then, just as I was about to lose consciousness I felt myself being beamed out of the water and onto a starship.

"What a great death," I was thinking when I felt as if some one else slipped into my body. I heard the voice say, "I am not *some one else*. I am you in a higher frequency reality."

My eyes flew open, but instead of being on a ship I was on the flat rock from which we often dove into the lake. Because of my multidimensional consciousness I could see two simultaneous versions of that event.

One was being beamed onto the ship, and the other was that my older brother had seen what had happened, swam across the lake and pulled me toward the rock for his friend to pull me out of the water.

I remember how I was freezing and that it took a long time for them to make me cough and throw up the water. I then heard the ambulance that someone had called. I had spent a long time in the hospital as I became very sick after that incident. In fact, I was somewhat of an invalid for several years.

I could never do athletics as I easily "ran out of breath." All my life I had looked at my "drowning" as the worst thing that could have happened. Now I realize that it was the best thing that had happened. If I had not been sick for so long, I would never have read all those metaphysical and science *fiction* books.

Also, I likely would not have met my "invisible friend" who was with me until I became a teenager. Of course, I quickly forgot the higher dimensional component of Mytre beaming me onto the Ship and steeping into me. Now I realize that my invisible friend was actually my own higher self, Mytre.

No wonder I recognized Mytre, as he was the one who entered my body. But how could he be inside of me and also be in all the other places such as the Pleiades and the Arcturian Mothership?

"I will happily answer all your questions," said Mytre responding to my thoughts.

"Since you are me, I guess you can easily read my mind," I said.

"It is not as simple as 'I am you.' It is more like 'we are ONE.' Do you understand what I mean?" asked Mytre. He was speaking telepathically, but I was hearing him perfectly.

"Yes, I think I understand what you mean, sort of. Do you mean that in a higher dimension you and I are ONE?"

"That is a good place to start." He smiled as he patted me on the back. I could not remember ever being patted on the back in that manner. I could never be a *jock* because of my ill health, which pretty much recovered as an early adult. However, my experience had left me shy and insecure.

Only Sandy could look into my heart to see my true self. My older brother who saved my life was killed a few years later in a car crash, which made me believe that he somehow had to sacrifice his life to save mine.

"You will meet the one who was your brother on the Ship," Mytre again responded to my thoughts.

At this point I could take no more and burst into tears. To see my brother alive! To know that he, too, was Pleiadian released me from a lifetime of guilt believing that I had taken his life away from him. Sandy rushed across the scout ship to embrace me, and I actually allowed her to comfort me.

In fact, I realized that that was the first time since my "drowning" that I had allowed anyone to deeply comfort me. When my brother died, I was stoic and could never cry. Now I cried for all the years that I could not cry before.

After what seemed like forever, but was actually "beyond time," I began to feel the same peace and calm that I did when I was dying, but now these feelings were because I was alive.

SANDY SPEAKS:

My experience was not as dramatic as Jason's. Maybe that was because I was thinking about helping him more than thinking about what was really happening. Either way, by the time Jason had regained his center, I had fully adjusted to our situation. In fact, I wondered why I was so calm. It even felt normal, as if I had finally come *home* after a long journey.

Yes, that was it. This event was a homecoming for me. I had never felt at home in the physical plane. Fortunately, I had my invisible friend who talked to me like I was an adult rather than a kid. My invisible friend woke me up when my nightly nightmares became too scary and taught me mind control as a teen so that I could control my thoughts even while asleep.

Most importantly, my invisible friend listened to me while I complained about my life. I did not have a family in which it was safe to be my real self. Therefore, I developed a "not me" persona so that I could communicate with the strangers that appeared to be my earth family. Then I would retire to my room, lie on my bed, look up to the ceiling and talk to my invisible friend.

"Do you mean the Arcturian?" said Mytria responding to my thoughts.

"What!" I said in shocked voice. "Was I talking to the Arcturian all that time?"

Suddenly, the small ship was filled with the familiar light and feel of my invisible friend. Instantly, I calmed down and allowed the light to embrace and comfort me. My invisible friend had returned.

I had been so distracted by falling in love with Jason and all of our great adventures that I had not even thought of my dearest friend. How could I desert my lifelong comforter?

"You never deserted me," spoke the familiar voice of the Arcturian. "You just pulled me inside of *our* joined Oneness."

Mytria responded to my shocked look by saying, "Yes, dear, that is the voice of the Arcturian. It is here with us now."

Now it was my turn to cry, but my tears were those of joy rather than sadness. Mytria embraced me and said, "Yes, the Arcturian has always been OUR guide and comforter."

"Our?" I asked through my tears. Of course, just as Mytre was Jason's higher expressions, Mytria was my higher expression. Jason and I had considered that fact before, but our human modesty did not allow us to recognize our own higher expressions of SELF.

"Wait, if Mytria and Mytre are us, and they are Divine Complements, does that mean that Jason and I are Divine Complements?" I accidently said out loud.

"Yes," Mytria and Mytre said in one voice. "Now that you have both merged with us, all four of us will merge with our joint higher expression, the Arcturian."

Jason and I were startled by their comment, but we managed to accept their outstretched hands. Mytre and Mytria held hands while Jason took Mytria's hand and I took Mytre's hand. In this manner the four of us created a circle.

Jason and I had been told that we were all ONE, but NOW we could FEEL that Oneness. As soon as Jason and I relaxed into the overwhelming sensation of our joint energy, the Arcturian filled the center of our circle.

The feelings of euphoria, bliss and unconditional love filled our circle of light and penetrated deep into our core. Instantly, we felt ourselves being transported back to the core of Gaia.

The Lemurians had prepared a great celebration with wonderful music and delicious food. Everyone was beaming with joy and unconditional love.

"Welcome," said Lantern who walked right over to greet us. "First we will hear a short message from our dear Arcturian friend."

Changing Realities Part 3

The Arcturian's Message

THE ARCTURIAN SPEAKS:

When Sandy and Jason were first beamed to the Lemurian settlement in Inner Earth their Lightbodies were eighty-three percent activated. This percentage of activation was mostly because they were bonded with each other, as well as with their higher expressions of Mytria, Mytre and Mytrian.

However, as they entered the beautifully decorated and highly attended celebration given in their honor, they became intimidated and their consciousness dropped. Instantly, Mytre merged with Jason while Mytria merged with Sandy to assist them to adapt to the honor that was being bestowed on them.

When Lantern saw that Sandy and Jason needed some "time" to adapt to yet another new experience, he called a few Lemurians to guide them to their seats and provide them one of their wonderful sparkling beverages and delicious fruit. Sandy and Jason, who were now able to hold their humanoid own forms again, were happily visiting with the friendly Lemurians.

Once the multidimensional crowd of visitors found their seats and settled in to receive our message, we beamed our unconditional love into the expansive room. Instantly, the room became quiet, calm and centered within our Arcturian energy field, and we began our message.

"Dearest August Members of Gaia's Planet Earth," we began. "We will speak to you in the same manner as we will speak to the topsider humans. As many of you know, when the Galactics land on Gaia's surface, you, the members of Inner Earth, will send your emissaries topside to assist and educate the many humans who will be dazed and confused.

"With that said, we will continue speaking to you, our dear Lemurian friends, as if you were the very humans that you will be going topside to support. In this way we will guide you in the same manner that you will guide the topsider humans.

"Dear Human Representatives for Gaia, we come to you within this NOW to tell about Earth's earliest history. The seeding of a planet is much like the seeding of the ground. Seeds are planted in the hope that they will grow and prosper.

"In the same fashion, beings from different planets, galaxies and dimensions planted their "seeds" in the hope that they could live, grow and prosper on a young (in planetary terms) world. However, rather than physical seeds, we Galactics planted seeds of consciousness.

"We, the Arcturians, were among the first Galactics to send our seeds of consciousness into the life forms of planet Earth. Hence, it is we who have come to you to deliver this message. We encourage all of you to remember your Galactic Family.

"Those of you who have taken incarnations on surface Earth will need to dust off the cobwebs of forgetfulness from your incarnations during the Piscean Age. During that age of the Kali Yuga, which is referred to as the Dark Age, humanity was as far away from the ONE as possible.

"In fact, humans believed that the Sun revolved around the Earth, and that the Earth was the most evolved planet in all of the Galaxy, or even the Universe. It takes a strong person to recognize they were mistaken in their perception of reality. It takes an even stronger person to recognize the many lies that have limited their expansion into SELF.

"Most important, it is your NOW to release your fear of other civilizations. We come to remind you that you have many expressions of your Multidimensional SELF who are currently holding forms on Starships, on different planets and in different galaxies.

"Most of your galactic expressions live in fifth dimensional light bodies that exist within the NOW of unconditional love. However, there are still some members of the Power Over Others galactic worlds that exist on the third/fourth dimension of our Galaxy, as well as on Earth.

"Most of these beings have changed their ways once they finally lost The Galactic War. However, many Draconians came to Earth after they lost the war. The Draconians are the descendants of the great dinosaurs of Earth's ancient history. Therefore, they believe that Earth is their planet.

"These beings are primarily responsible for the fall of Lemuria and Atlantis, as well as many of the wars your planet has suffered. However, their reign has come to an end. Because of their resistance to unconditional love, their resonance is unable to expand into the fifth-dimensional lightbodies that will inhabit Gaia's new fifth dimensional Earth.

"Fortunately, just as some members of these civilizations remained lost to the darkness of 'power-over-others,' there were others who ascended into the fifth dimension. Some of them took refuge in the earth, such as your selves, to await their opportunity to ascend themselves *and* planet Earth. Therefore, do not judge another by their species or the habits of their greater family. All life has an opportunity to join Gaia on New Earth, and all life will be welcomed.

"Many, such as this gathering of Lemurians, live just one half octave above the physical world on Earth's surface. You, our dear Lemurian friend, entered Earth before She plummeted into Her lowest frequency.

"Because of the completion of the great cycle of the Procession of the Equinox, Earth is now in alignment with the Galactic Center. Thus, the planet's frequency of resonance is slowly *and* surely rising.

"In fact, Earth entered Her Golden Age in late 2012 and She will remain in this era for 2,000 years. During these 2,000 years, multidimensional light and unconditional love will flow directly from the Galactic Center and into the heart of Gaia. Hence, it is the NOW for transmutation of Gaia and ALL Her inhabitants.

"Gaia is ready NOW, as is her plant and animal kingdom. It is humanity that is still attached to the 3D Matrix and cannot look beyond it. Fortunately, there are also many humans who are fully prepared to transmute into the higher frequencies of reality. Dear members of Inner Earth, when you go topside, your first assignment is to find these fully awakened ones.

"Then, just as we talk to them when we bring them on our Ships, you can talk to them as they walk the body of beloved Gaia. You may wonder when all this will occur, so allow us to answer this question. All that we have spoken of will occur not at a given time, but in a given frequency.

"The number of humans who can perceive this frequency, which is of course the resonance of the fifth dimension, is expanding exponentially. Therefore, we ask once again, be patient within your NOW. Cherish every moment of the life you NOW live. In this moment you live in unconditional love, which is the key to your transmutation into your fifth dimensional Lightbody.

"Blessings dear Ones. When we say we are WITH you, we mean we are IN you, just as you are IN unity with us."

When we finished our message, the room was totally quiet. We knew that the task of going topside to try to communicate with the third-dimensional humans was daunting to them. Therefore, we continued.

"Yes, our dear friends. Humanity has been lost in the illusions of the third dimension since the fall of Atlantis. We know that you are impatient for their awakening, but remember that you have been living in the fifth-dimensional pocket of Gaia's heart.

"Do you remember when the Atlantians destroyed your world? Do you remember the great fear that you felt and the anger that filled your hearts regarding the Atlantians? The topsider humans have been experiencing this degree of fear and anger since the fall of Atlantis.

We send a wave of unconditional love into this audience again to open their hearts and minds to more information. When we felt their confusion and worry transmute to love and dedication to purpose, we continued.

"Lemuria and Atlantis were meant to

bring Gaia into a dualistic reality so that Gaia could serve as a school in which beings could incarnate to learn the Law of Cause and Effect. This law was to be taught to the students (inhabitants of Earth) by giving them "time" between the energy field going out into reality (cause) and when it returned back to the sender (the effect).

"In a unified, fifth dimensional reality, cause and effect occur instantly. Hence, Gaia chose to resonate to the frequency of the third dimension. To do so, she had to lower her resonance from the NOW of the fifth dimension and beyond into the time-bound resonance of the third dimension of duality.

"Since time is created by polarities such as male/female, good/bad, day/night, Gaia would need to have male and female inhabitants. Lemuria was to be the female 'Mother Civilization' to represent the Flow of the electron, receptive/inflow, feminine polarity of energy, experienced as love and emotions.

"Lemuria began when life on planet Earth was in its infant stages, and the 'mothers' loved the infant planet by merging with the elements of the earth, air, fire and water. You Lemurians had no desire to become an individual or to 'think' about having personal power. You saw yourselves as one with all life on Earth.

"Atlantis, on the other hand, was to be the 'Father Civilization' and was meant to represent the Flow of the proton, expressive/outflow, masculine polarity of energy, experienced as power and thoughts. The Atlantians enjoyed thinking and discovering how they could change and improve their world.

"Whereas your Lemurian spirituality was based on love of all life and Mother Earth was your divine leader, the Atlantians looked upwards into the sky. They could understand and conquer the land and sea, but they could not, yet, understand and conquer the sky. Therefore, their spiritual guidance came from far above them.

"Are you beginning to see how polarity began to take hold on Gaia's planet?" we asked and observed as they shook their heads yes.

"Through the marriage of feminine, *Love/Emotion* and the masculine, *Power/Thoughts*, the two landed expressions of Gaia could gain the great *Wisdom* to combine their thoughts and emotions to create a beautiful reality in which everyone could learn by putting together what had been separated.

"When the humanoids, the Keepers of

the Land, could unite their thoughts and emotions (masculine and feminine) they would create their new world. Unfortunately, instead of a beautiful bonding and resulting ascension, their "marriage," like many Earthly marriages, ended in a long "divorce" in which both of them lost everything.

"Part of the reason for this *divorce* of power and love was that the 'power-over' galactic ancestors of these great civilizations could never approve of this marriage. All they wanted was to 'have it ALL.' In other words, greed was the cause of destruction then, just as it is in your NOW.

Since Gaia is NOW in the energy field of galactic light and planetary unity, the marriage of ALL polarities into the ONE is the hope and means of ascension. As we tell the age-old story of love and power, peak and fall, unity and separation, we ask you to listen with your Multidimensional SELF, so that you will remember YOUR Truth.

"Through remembering your own Truth, your own perception of this story, you can take that which was in your distant past and bring it into your present to create a future of ascension within the NOW of the ONE. In this manner, you can travel in consciousness via the oscillation of the sine waves of your consciousness. The higher your consciousness, the faster the oscillation of sine waves, and the more quickly you will travel inter-dimensionally via your consciousness.

"The frequency of your consciousness is influenced by the rate of the spin of molecules within your form. If your form resonates to a much lower frequency than your multidimensional consciousness, your consciousness and form will not be in entrainment. Therefore, you will *not* be able to perceive what is occurring within your higher frequency consciousness and inter-dimensional travels.

"It is the discrepancy between the frequency of your form and the frequency of your consciousness that creates the illusion of separation in which you feel separate from your Multidimensional SELF. In the world in which humanity has lived since before the fall of Atlantis, this type of "separation from SELF" was unknown.

"Before the fall of Lemuria, and even until the later times of Atlantis, the humanoid form resonated to the fifth dimension and beyond. Because of these high frequencies, the bodies did not have a static form. In fact, many did not need a form at all and existed as pure consciousness.

"Through the early and positive actions of the early Atlantians, Spirit can now inhabit the fourth dimension. It is the challenge of the grounded ones, who are the descendants of Atlantis, to bring Spirit into the matter of the third dimension.

"The Atlantians created this splitting of their spiritual and denser forms when they began genetic engineering. Before the genetic engineering, all forms on Atlantis were 'visited' by androgynous Spirits of the higher dimensions. These spiritual beings *visited* Atlantis in the same manner that you would log in to a video game.

"Life for most of the Lemurian era and a lesser portion of the Atlantian era was exactly like logging into a 3D video game. The higher dimensional Spirits entered into a form that was clearly a 'game' on the holographic matrix of fourth dimensional Earth. At first, they entered the plants and animals. Humans were so un-evolved at that time that there was little differentiation between a human and any other form of animal.

"Humans were male and female just like the other third dimensional *animals*. Visitors from other Star Systems who were in need of biped workers had genetically engineered these 'humanoid animals' millennia before. However, the early Atlantians, as well as the Lemurians, were androgynous and visited earthly forms to temporarily experience the concept of gender.

"Due to the actions of the later day Atlantians, the Spirit's state of consciousness lowered, and they suffered an increasing sense of separation from the higher dimensional expressions of their Multidimensional SELF. Eventually, their consciousness lowered so drastically that the oscillation of the sine waves of their consciousness slowed to such a low frequency that they could no longer travel inter-dimensionally. Then they became trapped in the forms that they were once just "visiting."

"Travel via consciousness is based on the oscillation of the sine waves of the traveler's consciousness. The higher the consciousness and the faster the spin and oscillation, the more easily the Spirit (true non-physical form) can travel inter-dimensionally via consciousness.

"Because the frequency of consciousness is influenced by the rate of spin of molecules within the form that Spirit is visiting, it became increasingly difficult for the visiting Spirits to remember their true consciousness while they were inhabiting a denser form.

"For many millennia, Spirits visited the third/fourth dimensional reality in which the masculine and feminine polarities were separated into two different genders. These visits became longer and longer as the Spirits became addicted to the experience of lower dimensional form. These longer visits into the increasing sensation of "time" on Earth further lowered the Sprits consciousness.

"When the frequency of their consciousness dropped to the frequency of the form they were visiting, they were no longer Spirit visiting form, but Spirits trapped in form. The trapped Spirits then knew the experience of death, which was never experienced when they were Spirit because they lived infinitely while within the unity of the ONE.

"Worse yet, the Spirits trapped in Atlantian form did not take responsibility for the creation of their own problem. Instead, they blamed the ONE for punishing them and making them stay within their decaying, dying earthen vessels. Therefore, they separated themselves from the ONE as well as from their own Spirit within their physical forms.

"Eventually, they even polarized the ONE into gender deities of God or Goddess. This final separation from the ONE cemented their fate into the long decline into beings of form rather than beings of Spirit. Spirit was always within them, but they had evicted it from their minds.

"Hence, they could no longer experience their own spirit through their physical perceptions. For this reason, their inner Spirit became a distant hierarchical ruler who was either a male "God," or a female "Goddess." Once Spirit became polarized in their consciousness, the battle between God and Goddess was focused on the battle between female Lemuria and male Atlantis.

"Lemuria and Atlantis had peacefully co-existed for millions of years, but the Atlantians were conflicted and needed to vent that anger onto others. Therefore, that which was meant to be the blissful marriage of masculine and feminine that would return Earth into Her Spirit form and usher in personal and planetary ascension became a long and violent divorce."

We could see that the audience needed a break to absorb our message, so we called in the musicians to play and invited the group converse with each other over some food and sparkling drinks. In this manner they could more easily integrate our information into their consciousness.

Changing Realities Part 4

Gaia's message

THE ARCTURIAN CONTINUES:
After our audience had a chance to relax, converse, and have some delicious food, we can forward again to complete our message.

"Our dear friends and family, we are pleased to see how you have all blended into ONE group of conscious volunteers to assist Gaia. We wish to finish our message and then invite a very important being to speak.

Once the group had settled down and were prepared to listen to our message, we began our message, "In summary, we reiterate that Lemuria was to be the matrix for the feminine, receptive, emotive and creative aspect of the future humanity. On the other hand, Atlantis was meant to be the masculine, logical and scientific aspect of future humanity. Both of these realties fell from resonating to the fifth dimension to a frequency that we would now call the fourth dimension.

"It was not within the Divine Plan to create a reality at the third dimension, for the separation from Spirit would make future evolution too difficult. Unfortunately, after the fall of these two great worlds, especially the fall of Atlantis, Earth was so shaken on her axis that Earth was in danger of total destruction.

"Therefore, Gaia called out to Spirit to send light beings to assist Her, as she was on the edge of falling off her axis. Millions of loving light beings took forms made of the same elements as Gaia. They hoped that if they could transmute the lower dimensional forms into a higher frequency, they would be able to assist Gaia to do the same. However, Earth was too wounded to resonate any higher than the third dimension.

"Even though Gaia's consciousness resonated to the fourth dimension, Her planetary body needed eons of healing before it could also resonate to the fourth dimension. It was then that the fourth dimension became the reality that vibrated in the aura of Gaia and She became separate form -Her planetary body that resonated to the third dimension.

"The creators of the Earth experiment were very concerned about the absence of Spirit's integration into third-dimensional matter. They knew that matter separated from Spirit would create a very harsh world that would become increasingly polarized. It is the presence and frequency of Spirit that allows all life forms on, in and above Earth to find and live within the unity of Planetary Consciousness.

"In a reality devoid of Unity and Planetary Consciousness, the grounded humans experience extremes of separation from each other and from their planet. In an attempt to make sense of their difficult lives, the ones who fell into darkness grew to believe that whatever they *did* was good for others.

"With such separation from Spirit, the light ones tainted their unconditional love of the ONE with the *conditional* love of their polarized reality in which others had to follow their commands to *deserve* love. This manner of separation of unconditional love and conditional love began in Atlantis while Lemuria was still in existence.

"The Atlantians increasing separation from spirit created a 'conditional love,' in which only those who followed their choices *deserved* to be loved. This conditional love set them on a mental/masculine path to gain *power over* others. Worse yet, the "others" included the planet itself. On the other hand, Lemuria's 'unconditional love' became so polarized to the emotional/feminine that they began to perceive what they wanted to see rather than which was actually occurring. Hence, they did not see that the Atlantian power systems were being used as weapons. In the end, both civilizations perished, but much was learned.

"From this experiment of polarized reality on Earth, it was learned the mental, masculine quality and the emotional, feminine qualities had to blend in order to gain sufficient wisdom, power and love. Hence, the Three Fold Flame of Wisdom, Power, and Love were placed in the High Hearts of all incarnating ones.

"Unfortunately, in most cases, this correction was useless. After the fall of Atlantis the frequency of Gaia's body was so low that most humans were unable to connect with their High Heart. Hence, much of their lives were spent in the business of survival.

"The Priests and Priestesses of the ONE carried their Light with them into the new locations to which they fled. Unfortunately, many of those who thrived on separation took the darkness of power-over others into the same locations. Thus, the battle between light and dark was carried into the surviving realities. This battle cannot be won. But it can be ended. Like any fire, it must have fuel to burn.

"As humanity begins to release their habit of third-dimensional time, they will begin to live In the NOW. Within that NOW, they will remember that they are NOT the body that has a spirit high above them. Gradually or quickly they will remember that THEY are the spirit that has chosen to visit the body.

"It is then that they can learn the law of cause and effect so that they can become the creators of their lives. The cause of creation is sent out into reality as a *thought*, it instantly merges with an *emotion*, to create a *thought form*. By placing their attention on that thought form, they consciously enter that reality.

"When they are complete with that experience, they release the thoughts and emotions that bonded them to that reality and return back to the NOW of the fifth dimension and beyond.

"As more and more humans remember that they are the creators of their life, they can experience any dimension they choose by calibrating their consciousness to frequency of that dimension. When this occurs, they will likely log out of the third/fourth dimensional portions of Earth's planetary matrix. Eventually, this lowest frequency of Gaia's matrix will become obsolete.

"Gradually, this frequency of Gaia's multidimensional matrix will dissolve because there are not enough thoughts and emotions to keep it in form. Therefore, there will no longer be a third/fourth dimensional matrix onto which life forms can attach.

"Thus, the third/fourth dimensional timelines, along with those inhabitants, will expand into a higher frequency OR move into the matrix of another third/fourth dimensional planet. In this manner, those who are not yet complete with the experience of resonating to third/fourth dimensional realities will simply switch into another reality as easily as one can switch into a different dream.

"With the recalibration of Gaia's planetary resonance, the portals into the fifth dimensional matrix of New Earth will gradually open. There is no need for disaster or confusion. As the portals into multidimensional Earth steadily open, those who choose to remain on a third/fourth dimensional planet will unconsciously be re-routed to other physical planets that are experimenting with the concept of polarity and separation. There is no judgment of 'success or failure' in these choices.

"Much can be learned from living in the separation, limitation and the extremes of polarity. Each being will make their decisions based on their own Divine Path. In fact, there are some higher dimensional beings that have chosen to remain in the lower dimensions to assist those who still believe they are *only* physical.

"We have come here within the NOW to celebrate that the ascension of Gaia is about to begin. As you Lemurians know, the shift of frequency of an entire planet is not a quick fix. Instead, planetary ascension is a process that will continue for as long as the planetary inhabitants are still attached to time.

"It is for this reason that many members of our galactic family have taken a human form and you, dear Lemurians, will slowly go topside to assist humanity with their decisions. Please be aware that your civilization was reticent to change. Hence, your ancestors did not see the brewing storm on Atlantis. Therefore, you are perfect teacher for the humans who do not want to even imagine that their world could completely change.

"Many members of our Galactic Federation have begun our 'landings' on Earth by bi-locating into the bodies of our expressions of SELF wearing an earth vessel. You, the Lemurians, will journey topside to teach, comfort and guide the humans through your ability to transmute your form to look like you are 'just human.'

"We conclude our transmission as we have two very special guests.

"We are the Arcturians. Sending our blessings to you all."

JASON SPEAKS:

When the Arcturian completed Its message, all Lemurians, Atlantians, humans and Galactic, stood up and toned in the manner which was Inner Earth's version of applause. The toning was so powerful that the entire room and all the beings and objects within it began to glimmer with an ever-increasing golden light.

Sandy and I were so overwhelmed by this energy field of light that we began to morph in and out of form. First our form appeared human, then it became a cloud of light like the Arcturian's formless form, then it took on the tall, thin shape of the Lemurians, the shorter but more humanoid shape of the Atlantians.

We also found ourselves wearing the forms of Mytre and Mytria, as well as our composite form of Mytrian. Finally we rested into the shapes of Sandy and Jason.

"These are just a few of the myriad incarnations that you have experienced in your long excursion into form," said Mytre and

Mytria with one voice. Mytrian, who suddenly joined us, smiled in agreement.

We were about to ask for more information about our "excursions into form" when everyone in the room turned toward the side entrance of the room and became totally silent. When Sandy and I witnessed the tall, regal female of golden light, we had to resist the temptation to drop to our knees.

We did not know who this woman was, but she felt so familiar that it was as if we had always known her. Suddenly, we found ourselves standing directly in front of her. We had no idea why we should be transported to stand there, but we were deeply honored.

"It is Gaia. She has taken a human form!" we heard in hushed whispers from those behind us. Sandy and I both thought, as we dared not speak within this holy moment, "Gaia can take a human form?"

To our surprise, Gaia looked directly into our Soul and said, "Dear human warriors for the light, I AM *all* the forms on my planet."

Now we could NOT help ourselves and fell to our knees in front of Her.

"Rise," spoke Gaia in a heavenly voice that echoed through the large room. "It is I that has come here to honor you. Of course, I honor not just you two humans. I honor all humans who have openly embraced every challenge and energetic transition with love and courage. I have created this form so I could join you *all* as we celebrate *our* planetary ascension."

As Sandy and I bowed to Gaia again and slowly walked back to our chairs, we could feel the warm smiles of all the members of the room. We quietly sat down and tried to blend into the room.

Then, we watched in awe as the Arcturian flowed to face Gaia with a low, respectful bow. When the Arcturian rose to an upright, glimmering shape It merged with Gaia in a burst of light that expanded far beyond the room.

This light reflected the galactic light of distant worlds as well as the earthly light of dawn, high noon and sunset. Galactic and earthly light intermingled into the birthing reality of Gaia's return to Her higher expression of fifth-dimensional New Earth.

The Arcturian then stood beside and a bit behind Gaia as she said; "Within this room are members of Inner Earth, surface dwelling humans and humanity's Galactic ancestors united as ONE. I bask in the glory of this NOW. To see my many humanoid beings gathered together in peace and love fills me with joy and unconditional love.

Through The Portal

"I tire of my polarity and am ready to return to my true fifth-dimensional expression of Oneness with ALL life. The experiment of holding my form in the lower frequencies of third-dimensional form has been arduous and very damaging to my body. My plant and animal kingdoms have been decimated and my earth and air have been polluted beyond conception.

"Humanity, who was meant to be Keeper of the Land, was the cause of this destruction. Fortunately, they are awakening, but far too slowly. It is the NOW for my return to a frequency of life in which ALL the members of my planetary body can prosper and find peace and love. I am complete with the experiment of holding a form in such a low frequency that humanity battles each other while the innocent suffer.

"I see that within this room is the joining of my first inhabitants, Draconian, Pleiadian, Sirian and many others, who have moved on to become members of the Galactic Federation. I feel their Starships that wait within my atmosphere to assist those who are ready to remember their full Multidimensional SELF.

"I see the topsider humans who have remembered their heritage both in their earliest societies of Lemuria and Atlantis as well as their galactic heritage. Through this remembrance you, dear humans, are able to expand your multidimensional consciousness to experience being within my Core.

"And, of course, I thank the members of my dear friends of Inner Earth who have long awaited this time of joining. These Lemurians and Atlantians have, at last, learned to live in peace within my Inner Earth. I also thank my dear sister Venus and brother Mars who have surrounded and protected me through the long dark night of the Kali Yuga.

"I wish to thank all of you who are joined NOW within my core to welcome the New Age of Multidimensional Light and Unconditional Love."

As Gaia spoke Her body morphed into visions of glorious forests, clear and brilliant skies, immense oceans filled with life, vast prairies and tall mountain ranges. All of these visions overlapped and included Her humanoid form. When She completed her message, she returned to Her golden form.

Gaia stretched out her left arm and said, "I now introduce Sanat Kumara, who served for eons as my Planetary Logos. Without the protection and guardianship of this fully evolved and higher dimensional being, my planet would have perished long ago. To our surprise, Gaia knelt as Sanat Kumara entered the room.

Suzanne Lie, Ph.D.

Pleiadian Perspective on Ascension Book 5
Through The Portal

LEMURIAN LEADERSHIP

Lemurian Leadership Part 1

Sanat Kumara Speaks

SANAT KUMARA SPEAKS:

Beloved Ones, we speak *through* you as well as *to* you. We come into your NOW to assist you to remember what you learned on Venus before you took your first incarnations on Earth.

All of you in this HERE and NOW were among those who answered Gaia's call at the fall of Atlantis. You were such beings of light that you needed to go to Venus to lower your frequency to one that could step into a form on Gaia's gravely wounded planet.

It is not important whether or not you remember that journey. What we, Sanat Kumara, call into your remembrance NOW is the service you vowed to give. This service was to remember your SELF throughout myriad incarnations during the long dark night of the Kali Yuga, which you all did.

Life after life you tried to remember. Sometimes you could only remember as a child, and when you 'played' on the Earth you assisted Gaia to remember. You see now that Gaia is a living being and capable of creating any form She pleases.

You do not realize how much you helped Gaia by remembering your love for her planetary expression. It was your love of Her planet that assisted Her to heal Her planetary body. As humanity fell deeper and deeper into their separation consciousness, they perceived Gaia as a mass of rock that is *just a thing*.

They were proud that they were no longer so "superstitious" that they thought of the planet as a living being. Besides, if Gaia was a being, she was a female, and females were also treated very badly during the Kali Yuga.

In fact, every person, place and thing was treated very poorly and much damage was done to the frequency of Gaia. However, your great light healed that darkness in ways that you were never aware.

Because you loved Gaia, Her land, Her sea, Her plants, animals, humans and atmosphere, you assisted Her to keep her planetary body alive. Now both people and planet have gone through many initiations, and you are both prepared to expand your awareness into your personal and planetary Lightbodies.

I Sanat Kumara, as well as the original 144,000 who came with me to Earth long ago, have returned. We are here NOW to work with the current Planetary Logos, Ascended Master Kuthumi, to assist our dear Gaia's reunification with Her Multidimensional Planetary SELF.

You are all aware of Gaia's fourth dimensional plane, as you have often visited it in your dreams. Due to your sporadic flashes into Lightbody, many of you have also become aware of Gaia's fifth-dimensional New Earth. This Earth is not actually "new."

Fifth-dimensional Earth has always existed, but the members of Gaia's planet have been pulled into their lower frequency expressions. However, New Earth is by no means uninhabited.

Many of the plants and animals that have become "extinct" have actually returned to their innate higher frequency of resonance. You will also be pleased to see that many cetaceans and "ascended humans" also reside on New Earth.

Nevertheless, I ask you not to leave your physical form, but to expand your consciousness back into the fifth dimension to connect with many of your ascended expressions of SELF.

Yes, dear humans, most of you here in this NOW have had at least several experiences of ascension, which is why you have been chosen among the myriad volunteers to assist Gaia.

You will need to recover the memory of the sensation of transmuting beyond your 3D physical form, through your 4D astral form and into your 5D Lightbody. In order to recover this memory you will need to release your attachment to third dimensional "modesty." According to your third dimensional indoctrination, it is immodest to remember your true, Multidimensional SELF.

Hence, many of you will have difficulty releasing all the old limiting emotions and thoughts that bind you to your old manner of storing information. In order to return to whom you have always been you must release the old concept of modesty, which are actually versions of "not good enough."

You have long stored all information in a sequential, separate fashion. In order to merge with Multidimensional SELF, you must remember how to consciously access the fifth dimensional information that is stored in a flowing, intermingling fashion of movements, emotions, thoughts and sensations.

This information is stored in your multidimensional mind. Once you connect your physical brain with your multidimensional mind with your third dimensional brain, you will begin to connect with your true, Multidimensional SELF and perceive all reality from your multidimensional perception.

In other words, we are asking you to change your perceptions of what you have been taught to expect as ascension. In order to do so, you will need to release your 3D habits of seeing, hearing, reading and/or sharing information through your third dimensional thoughts and emotions. Instead, you will need to intimately bond with all life in an experiential manner and allow each inhabitant of Gaia to communicate with you in its own manner.

Many of you have learned how to communicate with animals and plants, as they are a component of your daily life. Now you must remember how to communicate with the insects, the fish, the birds and all life on Gaia. This type of communication will remind you how to communicate with the elements and fifth dimensional elementals of earth, air, fire, water and ether.

You will begin this communication not by humanity's habit of telling, but instead with your Lightbody's habit of listening. As you deeply listen to the world around you, you will gradually remember how to communicate with all life.

Manly of the "primitive" peoples have enjoyed this communication for ages, which they remembered from their Lemurian ancestors. As you learn to communicate with these members of Gaia's ecosystem, you will regain your awareness of communicating with the Crystal Kingdom.

Once you can communicate with Gaia's Crystal Ones, you will be ready to entrain your consciousness with the Core and Cornerstone Crystals so that you can work together to recalibrate Gaia's *baseline frequency* of expression.

Gaia has been trapped in the illusion of the third/fourth dimension since the fall of Atlantis and is enthusiastic to return to the multidimensional light and unconditional love of Her true Multidimensional Planet.

Before we speak further of our honored task, let us rejoice in the Oneness of Gaia's pending transmutation. We see the feast laid out on the tables, the musicians ready to play and the flasks of Gaia's purest water ready to be served. Therefore, I, Sanat Kumara say:

"Let the festivities begin!"

SANDY SPEAKS:

Through The Portal

After Sanat Kumara spoke everyone was quiet for a few minutes, but as the music started and the food and drinks were served, everyone began laughing, talking and having a good time. Since time in Inner Earth is so different, I have no idea how long we ate, watched the amazing Lemurian dancers, and joined the dancers.

It was as if what Sanat Kumara said was so immense that we all had to allow the information to sink into our consciousness. The concept of listening to all of life's earth, air, fire, water and ether was so beyond many of us that we almost ignored what he had said.

On the other hand, Jason and I noticed that when we drank the wonderful Lemurian spring water, we thought of the water as a living being. Also, when we ate the fresh vegetables that were lovingly grown by the Lemurians, we took a moment to thank them for giving us their nutrition.

The fire from the many candles seemed to speak to us as it flickered, almost in rhythm to the music, and the air that was filled with music and joyous conversations seemed to glisten and sparkle around us. In fact, we could feel that the ground on which we danced was alive.

As we listened to the earth, air, fire and water, we began to see the etheric elemental that represented and lived within all the physical elements. However, our pondering of these sensations was soon lost in the marvelous conversations we were having with those around us. Mytrian had introduced us to his friends, and we were invited to sit with them.

As we became increasingly involved with our new friends, we so moved into the NOW that we almost forgot what Sanat Kumara had said. Once we entered the dance floor and our new Lemurian friends showed us some Lemurian dances, we were totally engulfed in the joy of that moment.

Since time was difficult for us to measure without the rising and setting of a Sun, we had no idea how long we had been dancing when Lady Gaia stood and raised her hands. As if by magic everyone in the room stopped what they were doing and focused their attention on Gaia.

"Please return to your seats as Sanat Kumara has a closing message for you." Everyone calmly returned to their seats to prepare for the honor of another transmission from the great Planetary Logos, Sanat Kumara.

Through The Portal

"Beloved Ones of Earth," said Sanat Kumara in a voice that went straight into our hearts, "I am joyous that you have all so deeply enjoyed our meeting. I wish to give you a message now so that you can discuss it with your new and lifelong friends. When this celebration concludes I am sending all of you, Lemurians and Atlantians included, up to the surface of Gaia's great body for the period of one Earth year.

"If needed, I will create a holographic form for those of you who need a body that will allow you to fit in with the topside area to which I am sending you. I will make sure that all of you have everything that is necessary to live in comfort for your year on Gaia's surface. Within that year that you are topside, you will learn how to talk to all life. As I have said before, your learning to talk to life must begin by learning to listen.

"Begin with one element at a time, such as earth, or air, or fire, or water or ether. Please choose whatever order is best for you. Once you have learned to communicate with each element, add one more element at a time. Finally, you will remember how to listen, talk and communicate with all life. At this point, gather some personal crystals and establish a relationship with them, one-at-a-time.

"By the end of the year, which means nothing in the NOW of the ONE, you will return here and together we will calibrate the Core and Cornerstone crystals of Gaia. Are there any questions?"

The room was quite. How could any of us question the great Sanat Kumara? Jason and I looked at each other and silently held hands. We knew that whatever we did, we would do it together.

Gaia interrupted our moment of intimacy by saying, "Thank you my dear inhabitants. We turned our attention to Gaia as She continued, "Beloved Sanat Kumara and I take your silence as an agreement to fulfill this mission. We know that all of you will successfully fulfill your assigned task.

"We ask that you converse amongst yourselves, as this is to be a group endeavor. Then, please continue the festivities to complete your alliance in Unity Consciousness, which you will quickly expand into Planetary Consciousness."

Lemurian Leadership Part 2

A Morning Message

JASON SPEAKS:

I woke up in our bed wondering if the whole event of finding the fifth-dimensional airport, going into the core of Gaia, attending the Lemurian celebration and the messages from the Arcturian, Gaia and Sanat Kumara were a dream.

"NO," said Sandy who was still half asleep, "It was NOT a dream." She then sat up, looked straight into my eyes and said, "Was it?'

I wanted to answer her, but heard a sentence in my mind, which felt like it was from Mytre and ran to get my computer.

"Are you getting another message?" I heard Sandy's sleepy voice.

"Yes," I replied, "can't talk now."

I knew that Sandy would respect my wishes and would even help me to make sense of the jumbled messages that I had increasingly been receiving in the morning. I plugged in the computer and booted it up as I glanced as the pile of mail in front of our mail slot.

I was wondering how that much mail could accumulate when I saw the computer was ready. Just I was beginning to write, Sandy entered the room and said, "Would you like me to type while you channel the message?"

Since I already heard the first sentence in my mind and Sandy could type much faster, I gratefully said, "Yes, that would be wonderful."

Sandy immediately, sat down next to me, put the computer in her lap and said, "I'm ready."

Since I did not have to type I closed my eyes and allowed the first sentence to flow through me. Knowing that Sandy was typing my message allowed me to relax as I said:

"As your process of ascension progresses, the myriad aspects of your Multidimensional SELF merge as your many lives on countless timelines, worlds, galaxies and dimensions begin to connect like pearls on a necklace. These aspects of your Multidimensional SELF are the *pearls* and YOU are the *string*.

"When your physical world is too challenging, one expression of your Multidimensional SELF in one timeline is almost too much to handle. However, as you progressively live in *surrender* and allow the Oneness of the NOW to be revealed with your every breath, more and more aspects of your SELF come online in your ever-expanding multidimensional consciousness.

"With the knowledge and wisdom of higher and higher dimensional expressions of your SELF, you remember more about living in surrender. When you live in surrender, life is a holographic movie in which you are the primary character. This character that you are 'playing' has increasing wisdom, power and love as you increasingly connect with the ever-expanding reality of your Multidimensional SELF.

"All of these expressions of your SELF are within what you once thought of as an 'individual life.' Now you know that each individual storyline, life, specific incarnation is rich and challenging in its own unique way. As you consciously connect with more expressions of your Multidimensional SELF, you regain a conscious connection to the myriad worlds, planets, galaxies and dimensions to which these versions of your SELF resonate.

"Whenever you accept another aspect of your Multidimensional SELF into your conscious awareness, that self brings its entire stream of lives, realities and expressions on many planets, star systems, galaxies, and dimensions.

"If that is not enough, you also have parallel and alternate realities, as well as possible and probable realities that may or may not occur. All these lives are occurring *simultaneously* within the NOW of the ONE.

"Each of these apparently singular expressions has myriad expressions of SELF that live in countless realities with infinite potential. ALL of these expressions of your immense Multidimensional SELF are connected with each other. In fact, they are merged with each other.

"When two aspects of person and/or reality are *connected* they are attached, but when they are *merged* they overlap. Within the area that of overlap, the two seemingly separate persons, places or things are ONE. All these myriad realities and potentials within your Multidimensional SELF exist in different dimensions as well as in differing stages of formation.

"Only third/fourth dimensional realities are bound by time and separation. Fifth-dimensional experiences are free of the encumbrance of time. Each third/fourth dimensional reality is interacting in a 'time-dance' of potential, beginning, occurring, ending and concluding. These potential, beginning, occurring, ending and concluded realities are perceived as occurring NOW within the ONE of the fifth dimension and beyond. "Your Multidimensional SELF can *pop-in* or *exit* any reality as simply as opening or closing a window:

- Your *third dimensional self* perceives a reality as being physical and bound by sequential time.
- Your *fourth dimensional self* perceives a reality as being astral in which time shifts from past, present or future but is sequential within each timeline.
- Your *fifth dimensional SELF* perceives a reality filled with Lightbodies interacting within the HERE of the NOW.
- Your *sixth dimensional SELF* perceives the NOW of each reality from the perspective of the core light-matrix of every being and location.
- Your *seventh dimensional Oversoul SELF* simultaneously perceives the NOW of all the realities in which you have, are or will experience form as ONE ornate and complete "matrix of expressions."
- Your *eighth dimension and beyond SELF* is no longer bound by form and exists as

pure consciousness in different stages of returning to Source. All realities are perceived as fields of energy, which you influence with your force of unconditional love.

"Meanwhile, your third-dimensional expressions are having a difficult time experiencing *only* one reality at a time. How can your physical self connect with and understand these myriad phases of countless realities? This understanding has to do with how you store information in your brain, which works much like one of your computers.

"Do you remember how your early computers were limited to a small amount of information? You would have to print out the information or store it on physical disks so that your computer would not become overloaded. All of these copies and/or disks were third dimensional and each of them was separate.

"Each disk of information had to be stored in a physical place and categorized so that you could find it when you wanted to access that information. If you forgot where you had stored that information, it was very difficult to retrieve it. Sometimes you would have to go through each disk and/or printed copy in order to find what you needed.

"There is much more storage within your present day computers. Also, even if you are not good at organization, you can retrieve any information by writing it in the upper right hand corner of your computer. Not only does your present day computer store much more information, it can store infinite amounts of information by putting it into the 'Cloud.'

"The Cloud is huge, beyond your imagination and all the information stored there intermingles with the other information. You can easily find your own information by typing its title on your computer or other computerized device. The Cloud maintains everyone's anonymity, meets everyone needs and is automatically up-graded.

"Your Multidimensional Mind operates much like the Cloud. Just as many individuals gathered together to create the Cloud manner of storage, the many individuals within your Multidimensional SELF are working together to gather all the information about all the expressions of your infinite, multidimensional SELF in your version of the Cloud, which is your Multidimensional Mind.

"You can consider your Multidimensional Mind as a 'CLOUD of the NOW' where All information is stored in a non-manifest manner. When you access the *Cloud* of your

Multidimensional Mind you access *all* your own personal and collective information from all your realities. Everyone shares this Cloud/Multidimensional Mind, as it resonates to the fifth dimension, which is beyond time and/or separation.

"We are not advertising a new technology. We are reminding you that technology reflects how many humans are remembering that there is a place where everything is always stored. This *place* is your own Multidimensional Mind. As your personal consciousness expands to encompass your multidimensional consciousness, your third/fourth dimensional brain expands to encompass your Multidimensional Mind.

"Your Multidimensional Mind lives within Unity Consciousness with all the myriad expressions of your SELF, as well as with all life. When you remember to access your Multidimensional Mind, you can gain answers to everything that you have ever experienced in any reality and any version of your Multidimensional SELF.

"Your challenge is to release the third-dimensional thoughts and the emotions that bind you to your third-dimensional thinking. You may ask, 'Do I release my 3D thoughts first or my 3D emotions first?' The answer to that question is, 'Any either/or thinking binds you to your third-dimensional brain.'

"Thoughts and emotions interact in a constant dance of creation and manifestation. When you remember that all your thoughts and emotions are expressions of your state of consciousness, it will become increasingly easier to calibrate your listening to the frequency of the SELF who is communicating.

"When you remember how to listen to ALL frequencies of your SELF, you will remember how to listen to ALL the frequencies of the life around you. For example, if you can listen to your own fifth dimensional SELF, you will be able to communicate with the fifth-dimensional elementals.

"When you listen with your fourth-dimensional emotions you will be more able to hear the aura of the plants and animals around you. When you can consciously 'listen to all life,' you move into the 'unity with all life' of your innate fifth-dimensional consciousness.

"It is not an easy task for a 'modern' human to allow a humming bird to tell you why it chose that flower or listen to the flower that the humming bird has chosen. You may find that it is easier to begin communication with all life via the fifth-dimensional unity consciousness of your Multidimensional Mind. You can begin with your fourth-dimensional meditations and dreams that will assist you to remember how to commune with all life.

"Whatever your state of consciousness, please remember that the greatest leaders are the servants to all that they lead. As you travel around your area, see not how each area is different. Instead, realize how each area of Gaia's beautiful body is united within the ONE of Her Being.

"Just as your hands, feet, voice, hearing, seeing, digestion, breathing, thinking, feeling etc. appear to be separate they are all a component of YOU. In the same manner, all the different areas that you will visit, commune with, bless and transmute are components of Gaia's Oneness."

When I finished my channel, I opened my eyes and looked over to see that Sandy was in a deep trance. Her eyes were closed and she was typing faster than I had ever seen. It almost looked as if her hands were flying just above the keyboard. I, too, closed my eyes, sent her my love and silently listened to quiet clicking of the keyboard.

When she finished typing, she was so exhausted that all she could do was hand the computer to me. I did not want to disturb the moment, so I scrolled to the top of the message and began reading out loud.

Suzanne Lie, Ph.D.

Lemurian Leadership Part 3

Communicating with all life

JASON READS:

"Reality is in layers of frequencies that are embedded on the holographic projections of 3D and 4D Earth. Your difficulties on these levels of reality have to do with the frequency of reality to which each of you are attuned.

"If you look at the fourth-dimensional lower astral plane and the lower survival levels of the third-dimension, you can see that the darkness is still in control on those layers of reality.

"In fact, many of those who desire *power-over others* have migrated to these lower levels of reality because they cannot tolerate the higher light that is flowing deeper and deeper into Gaia's third and fourth dimensional layers of reality.

"Meanwhile, more and more of you, including Gaia Herself, are moving into the higher frequency layers of reality in which energy out *quickly* returns as energy back. Those ruled by fear and anger and power-over-others are quite terrified about having the energy they send out being quickly returned.

"On some level of their unconscious self, they know the energy they have put out into the world and do NOT want to experience it coming back to them. The selfishness, the taking from others, the power over and the fear lived as anger and domination is not something they want to experience in *their* lives.

"Therefore they seek refuge in lower frequency layers of reality where energy out does not come back for a long time. There they rule over those who also live within that lowest frequency of reality.

"To live beyond the lower frequencies of reality you need to release the third-dimensional concepts of what is important. Very often, you need to release your attachment to money, as money has become a negative force on physical Earth. Money has been the reason for murders, wars, domination and selfish power-over others.

"Money is absolutely not a component of the higher fourth dimensional or fifth dimensional layers of reality. In fact, except in the lower astral, money is barely a component of the fourth dimension. As you expand your consciousness higher and higher, you release the third-dimensional concept of *hard work to get money* so that you can "have" enough or have "more."

"Something interesting is occurring in that often the ones that want money the most are the ones in the lower frequencies, which are ruled by the cabal. The cabal does not want others to get money, as that is a threat to them. On the other hand, as your frequency of consciousness raises, you can understand the false power of money because you are living more and more within the flow of *now of the one*. Hence, you increasingly release your needs and desires for money.

"Within this *flow* of the higher frequency layers of Earth, you are discovering your own inner-powers of creation. As you remember how to live within that *flow*, you move away from third-dimensional time and begin to live within the NOW.

"As you continue to naturally expand your consciousness into the realities that resonate beyond money, acquisition or power-over others your creativity expands and so does your freedom.

"More and more of you make this shift. Those who are still struggling and *working hard* will begin to wonder if perhaps they too could find out how to flow through life with peace and a sense of abundance.

"This abundance is not about money, or about the things that money can buy. This abundance is a state of mind that reminds you of your own ability to resonate to peace, love and happiness.

"As more people leave their corporate jobs, move out into the country, grow their own food, barter for what is needed, they will find that they are perfectly happy with less 'stuff.' These types of choices take down the cabal as quickly as the unconditional love that is being sent to them from the higher dimensions.

"What will happen when the tipping point is reached? What will happen when the majority of people think about Earth, other people and creativity, and the minority of people thinks about accumulation, success and power?

"When people are NOT lost in the struggle and dream of 'getting something,' they can more easily *flow* into the higher frequencies of reality that resonate beyond the illusion of needing more. Needing more is the opposite of being thankful.

"When you need more, you are affirming that there is 'not enough.' Then, your multidimensional, creative-self who resonates beyond the illusion of lack, hears, 'I am thinking about *not enough* and filling that thought with emotion. Therefore, please bring me more *not enough*.'

"Conversely, when you are thinking "thank you for the substance at hand" and fill that thought with emotion, your creative-self hears, "I am thinking about how thankful I am about the substance at hand," and brings you more of that for which you are thankful.

"The challenge for many of you is the rules of the 3D Game have changed and many of you *did not get the memo*. In the old version of the third-dimensional Earth you had to work hard to get ahead.

However, the 'old' third dimension has taken in so much higher light that instead of working *hard*, people are working *smart* to discover (which often means uncover) new (which means old and long hidden) technology that makes life so simple that they do not have to work at all.

"In other words, you are flowing into the NOW of New Earth! Just across the threshold to 5D New Earth, the Galactic Federation, who represents your ancestors and higher expressions of SELF, await your reunion. In this layer of reality money no longer exists, as it is no longer needed.

Through The Portal

"You all have replicators which can instantly create anything you need from food to furniture, personal tricorders/bio-scanners, voice recognition language translators, anti-gravity cars, etc. In fact, many of these devices are already invented right now in your present transitional reality.

"As you continue to flow into higher and higher frequency levels of New Earth, you will be seeing more and more of this technology in your daily life. This will occur because the dark ones who have been hiding this technology will no longer be able to resonate to that layer of reality. Therefore, the technology will be freely disseminated to everyone.

"As you move further into New Earth, which you are doing more and more each day, your Galactic family will come down from the sky and your Lemurian and Atlantian ancestors will come up from New Earth. They will move through your population assisting, loving and supporting all the newly awakened ones who have released their fear and turned towards love and creativity as a new way of life.

"At first you will move into and out of this layer of reality, as it will take practice and more mastery of your thoughts and emotions to maintain a constant presence in this frequency of New Earth. Your thoughts, emotions and bodily sensations will remind you that you have returned to the frequency of New Earth.

"Soon, you will remember how to maintain the state of consciousness in which you are Masters of your Energy Field. You do not need to learn or try or wait. Just expand your consciousness into the layer of reality in which you are a Master NOW and New Earth ALREADY exists.

"When you learned to walk, you often fell. When you learned to talk you said words wrong. You just had to practice, practice, practice and 'grow up.' You are all growing up now and returning to your Multidimensional SELF. Be as patient and loving with your self, as you would be with your beloved child. In fact, YOU are a beloved *Child of the Universe*.

"As the higher light infiltrates more and more of your reality, you will easily flow into higher and higher frequencies of reality to remember your true SELF and the Master that you already are! Know that what you have received is true. Feel it in your High Heart and accept it with your multidimensional mind."

"Sandy, this is an amazing message. Do you know who you were channeling?" I asked.

In a shy voice Sandy said, "I think it was Mytria."

I put down the computer I had been holding in my lap, stood up to walk to short distance to her side of the table and pulled Sandy to her feet. Once she was standing I held her so closely that we almost became the one person that I knew we already were!

Suzanne Lie, Ph.D.

Lemurian Leadership Part 4

Asking For Guidance

SANDY SPEAKS:

Jason and I were so excited that we got the assignment to visit other areas of Gaia and learn how to communicate with all life, including with the elements and elementals. Then, we both received amazing messages from our higher expressions of Mytre and Mytria. We were so happy that we were actually laughing and singing while we made breakfast, but when we sat down and started to eat, the reality of our new lives began to set in.

How could we possibly travel around the country? We could barely survive with our two jobs. Yes, we had changed our lives to find other ways to support ourselves, but travel is expensive and we had no extra money. This fact began to settle into our consciousness while we ate our first meal, in how long?

We had been jumping in and out of time so long that we could only guess at the time unless we looked at a clock. As the deep disappointment moved into my conscious awareness, I could feel myself starting to cry. I decided to excuse myself to *make some coffee*.

Through The Portal

I had just put the coffee in the filter when Jason walked into the kitchen looking as depressed as me. He announced that he did not want any coffee and was going to go out for a hike by himself. The hike by himself meant that he needed to think on his own, which was fine with me.

I, too, needed to work through this immense disappointment or, somehow, find a solution. I gave Jason a weak smile and a peck on the cheek.

"Yes, honey, a hike would be good for you now. I will straighten up and do these dishes."

Jason gave me a quick kiss on the forehead, went to our bedroom to put on his hiking clothes and was out of the door in less than ten minutes. I was relieved. "Now I can allow myself a pity-party," I thought as I straightened up the house, which was more like a one bedroom cabin. I cleared the dishes from the small table where we ate, worked and visited our friends. I then went over to the door, picked up the stack of mail and put it on the table.

I was trying NOT to do the female, crying thing, so I filled the sink with hot water and soap and put in the dirty dishes from the counter and from our breakfast. I knew some of them would have to soak for a while as they had been sitting on the counter for days.

How many days had we been away? Jason and I had not yet had the nerve to discover. We had crossed the threshold. We had not done our 3D jobs and would likely be fired. Even though we worked from home and were sort of "self- employed," we had duties, which we had not completed.

Now we could not even pay our rent, so I couldn't imagine how we could possibly travel around the countryside to *merge with the elementals*. I was so overwhelmed that I started to cry. Jason was gone, and I was alone so I mustered up the courage to call for assistance from our higher friends.

"Dear Higher Friends," I said, "Could I please ask you a personal question?"

I was flabbergasted when a huge cloud of sparking light entered my kitchen and condensed into a smaller, vaguely humanoid form standing next to me. It was the Arcturian! "Oh My God," I unconsciously exclaimed.

"We are here to answer your question," answered the Arcturian as it filled my aura with light. With this warm, Arcturian glow within me I asked a question that I did not even know that I had.

"Dear Arcturian, I am so honored that you have come to me. As you can see, I am experiencing many conflicting feelings that I need to understand. On the one hand I am very happy and peaceful, but on the other hand I am fearful about the many changes occurring within my self, my life and even the planet.

"I think it is the great pending *unknown* that is bothering me. I know that I need to leap into this unknown, but there are so many negative feelings that I am having - releasing (I hope) - about the third dimensional thought of… I am not sure of what.

"Maybe I am having thoughts of sorrow about certain things that I fear I will *not* experience. Yes, I think that may be it. As I think about it I realize that I am ready to go onto the next phase of my life, but without having to release this phase.

"I know I have been prepared to LET GO of that which I had thought of as important in my life. Yes, many of these things were indeed third dimensional. But they were not just things; there were also certain people.

"I must admit that sometimes the voice of my ego is louder than the voice of my true SELF. I wish to follow that higher voice and not the voice of my ego. On the other hand, the ego voice, or whatever inner-voice that has been bothering me, can be very loud. Perhaps it is my ego that is asking this question? Please assist me."

When I finally stopped talking, I could feel the tears streaming down my face. However, these tears we not tears of sorrow, but tears of release. I was ready to LET GO again, but this time I didn't even know of what. I had just begun to control my tears when the Arcturian moved forward to actually merge with my being.

Now I was sobbing. But it was not because I was sad. I was sobbing because I was so filled with unconditional love and joy that I could not contain it without releasing a lifetime of tears.

"Our dearest ONE," I could hear the Arcturian whisper into my consciousness, "We understand how difficult it can be for our Away Team during this major transition. Your society, world, frequency is at a very difficult point. The 'voice of change' is ever increasing, which serves to amplify the 'voice of fear.'

"Your myriad lives in a polarized reality have taught you that one extreme invites the other. Therefore, when you are at the peak of an experience, you are constantly reminded of the fear that it will somehow go wrong.

"The small things that have been *going wrong* arise from the creation of your unconscious self who is attempting to prepare you for failure. When you look into your life with your *eyes of fear* you see the many things that have gone wrong and dreams that have *not* been fulfilled.

"On the other hand, when you look into your life with the *eyes of love*, you can see the long-term accomplishments that you *have* fulfilled. We say fulfilled, because these accomplishments were not the result of your ego.

"Whether you know it or not, you have been following your inner guidance for all of your life. Hence, you have placed your self on the cliff where you feel like you must jump or languish in the old. The feeling of needing to *jump* is because you are following your inner voice.

"Your inner voice has given you assignments that are impossible for your third-dimensional thinking to understand. When you look back to who you were, then look at who you have become, you realize that your accomplishments have been under the guidance of your Higher SELF, which has primarily been us, the Arcturians."

"My Higher SELF is Arcturian?" I thought.

"We wish you to remember dear ONE," said the Arcturian responding to my thoughts, "YOU are a component of US. You are Arcturian, as well as a Pleiadian, and many other galactic expressions of SELF. How did the extremely shy and totally insecure child become the person you are today? It was because you listened to your inner voice.

"Right now, as with every transformational moment of your life, you are hearing two voices. You are hearing the *inner voice of your SELF,* and you are hearing the *inner voice of your frightened ego*. Your frightened ego is saying, 'Don't try it. You will fail.'

"When you also listen to the voice of your SELF you hear, 'You know that you have *failed* more times than you can count. However, EVERY time you dust off the failure and try again – and again – and again…until you finally succeed.'

"Do you see how brave you are that you do not give up on our SELF? Do you see how failure is a part of success? Every time you fail you learn something; that is you learn something *if* you listen to your SELF!

"Failure is not quitting. Failure is the beginning of a new task that you NOW feel strong enough to tackle.

"The fact that you are trying to do that which you were afraid to do before proves how courageous you have become. Remember, you have always asked your Higher SELF for assistance. Even if you only asked us in your night body and could not remember, you always sought our council.

"What is occurring within your NOW is that you are transmuting into a higher frequency of reality. Your third dimensional brain is overwhelmed by your multidimensional mind. Concepts, once hidden in doubt, are coming into the light of day to create bridges to connect these *islands of doubt* with *the highway of light*.

"The light of this highway is too bright to be perceived by your human perception. You must penetrate your doubt to find the way to open the truth you have hidden inside your doubt. You and Jason will be finding this inner truth when you commune with the earth, air, fire and water elementals.

"As you commune with the earth, air, fire and water around you, your inner elementals move into entrainment with what appears to be the outer elementals. You, and all life, are composed of physical atoms that are actually vortexes of energy, each one radiating to its own unique signature frequency.

"Your quantum physicists have discovered that physical atoms are made of vortices of energy that are constantly spinning and vibrating to their own signature frequency. If you observed an atom with a microscope, you would see a small invisible tornado-like vortex with a number of infinitely small, energy vortices called quarks and photons. All atoms are made of this invisible energy, NOT tangible matter.

"You see everything that humanity has called REAL is made of things that your third dimensional science has regarded as 'NOT real.' Physical matter really isn't physical at all. In fact, physical matter and consciousness are interwoven. When you observe an atom at its tiniest level, the behavior of that atom changes.

"From the higher dimensions, it is obvious that non-physical properties govern the universe and consciousness plays a vital role regarding the 'physical' make-up of your reality. Thus, as you radiate out the signature frequency of your consciousness, you influence the signature frequency of all the elements and elementals around you.

"Please remember that your signature frequency is determined by your state of consciousness. If you are trapped in a low frequency, fearful state of consciousness, you will entrain your signature frequency, as well as your perceptions, with those lower frequencies of reality.

"Since all matter is composed of fields of energy, which are easily affected by consciousness, your own physical matter is affected by the signature frequency of the elements and elementals that are within and around you. Thus, just as a beautiful flower, lovely sunset and clear sky makes your consciousness expand, dark concrete, human trash, and polluted sky lowers your consciousness.

"You are repetitively influencing your physical reality, and your physical reality is constantly influencing you. It is for this reason that so many ascending ones are leaving the crowded, polluted, concrete city to enter the countryside where nature's voice can be heard above the noise of the city.

"Since your consciousness is popping in and out of different states of consciousness, all of your atoms are constantly popping into and out of different frequencies via their minute vortices of focused energy. Meanwhile, YOU are popping in and out of myriad inter-dimensional travels.

"Do you understand now how the smallest impacts the largest, as well as the largest impacting the smallest? Most important, you are part of both the largest and the smallest.

"Your third-dimensional brain is not aware of these myriad journeys because it is bound by time. When you venture out of the physical, you move into the realities beyond time. Since your 3D brain cannot understand that concept, it merely ignores it. However, once your consciousness expands to include your multidimensional mind, you will begin to realize that you are actually going somewhere.

"However, you did not *go* some 'where.' You *go* to some 'frequency beyond the limitations of time.' When you are entrained with the surrounding fifth dimensional elementals, which resonate beyond time, your 3D brain can begin to recognize your brief moments of disconnections from time. That is all it can remember because your physical brain can only compute third dimensional perceptions and experiences.

"When you return, a second or two before or after you left, the fifth dimensional elementals with whom you have established a relationship, will remind the fifth-dimensional elementals inside your body that you have taken an inter-dimensional journey.

"To expand your relationship with the fifth dimensional elementals, first merge with the third dimensional elements of physical earth, air, fire and water. To further merge with the 3D elements, and hence the 5D elementals, look into the invisible element of *ether*.

"Within the surrounding ethers of your physical world are the many fourth dimensional portals to the realm of Faerie in which the fourth/fifth dimensional gnomes of the earth element, sylphs of the air element, salamanders of the fire element and undines of the water element reside.

"Children are often able to play with the faeries, gnomes, sylphs, salamander and undines in their imagination. Children, who have not yet forgotten their imagination, can expand their consciousness into the higher frequencies of reality by opening a portal between their third dimensional physical brain and their multidimensional mind via the highway of light, which is their imagination.

"When you become 'adults' you forget what you have always known because you have to *work hard* in a *job* to survive.

Fortunately, as you establish intimate relationships with the elementals, they will guide your multidimensional mind into the reality of your fifth-dimensional elemental self.

"It is through your relationship with the fifth-dimensional elemental world that you will KNOW Gaia as a living being of whom *you* are a component. This experience is similar to your toe realizing that it is part of your foot, which is part of your leg, which is part of your body and so on and so on.

"The greatest detriment to personal/planetary ascension is the illusion that you are separate from your reality. All the Lemurian descendants, as well as their descendants, your 'native peoples,' know that person and planet are ONE being. They know that they can influence their reality with their thoughts and have an intimate relationship with the elements and elementals.

"It is for this reason that each person, couple or small team that attended our Lemurian Celebration will be accompanied by a Lemurian. Their Lemurian friend will assist them to remember what they have *always* known. As you might guess, Lantern will be joining you and Jason.

"Be within the ONE. Maintain as high of a frequency of consciousness as possible and allow your life to unfold. YOU are the creator of your reality, so make sure that you allow your highest frequency of SELF to be the pilot your life.

"The higher the frequency of your consciousness, the higher the frequency of your creations. Furthermore, remember to *always* bless ALL fear with Unconditional Love to keep your consciousness and your creation filled with love and connected to the ONE!"

***

With these final words, the Arcturian disappeared from my vision, but not from my heart. I was wondering if I could remember everything so I could share it with Jason when I glanced at the kitchen door.

There was Jason looking at me with such love that my heart almost burst. He quickly walked the short distance across our small kitchen, encompassed me with his strong arms and whispered, "I heard everything!"

Suzanne Lie, Ph.D.

Pleiadian Perspective on Ascension Book 5
Through The Portal

BACK FROM LEMURIA

Back from Lemuria Part 1

Our New Life

SANDY SPEAKS:

After my meeting with the Arcturian, Jason guided me to the table and made some coffee so I could get more grounded. As I sat there waiting for my coffee, I started flipping through the stack of mail I had set on the table. After going through a bunch of bills we could not pay and a lot of junk mail, I came to a letter for Jason that was from a lawyer.

Obviously, the letter had followed him over several address changes and finally found its way to his current address. It looked like one of those envelopes that had a check in it, so I called Jason in to open it. He came in with our coffee and sat down to open the official looking letter.

"Oh," he said. "This was my rich uncle's attorney."

"You never told me about a rich uncle," I teased him as he opened the letter.

"Yes, he was a very nice man to me, but he offended just about everyone else he knew. However, he was very wealthy, so there were a lot of 'hanger-ons' who followed him around."

Then Jason's eyes became as big as saucers, and he took a deep breath, as he said, "He left me some money."

"Cool," I said. "Now maybe we can pay some of these bills."

"No," Jason said. "He left me a LOT of money. He left me enough money – such that we can buy this cabin, quit our meager jobs and, depending how we manage it, not work for years."

I was sure he was teasing me, so I laughed and said, "Yes, let's be wealthy 'lay-abouts.'"

"No," Jason exclaimed as he gave me the letter. "I am not teasing."

"When I read the letter, I almost fainted. All I could say was, "Wow, what are you going to do with all this money?"

Jason took my hand and looked into my eyes, "First I will marry you. Then we will take a year honeymoon to visit the elements and elementals."

All I really heard was the "marry me" part. "Marry me!" I said with such joy and surprise that he stood up, walked around the small table, pulled me up into a standing position and looked into my eyes as he said, "My dear Sandy, will you do me the honor of being my wife?"

I cannot express the joy and love that I felt in that moment. All I could do was shake my head up and down as I said, "Yes, oh yes, yes, yes, yes." We hugged each other tightly; then Jason picked me up and carried me into the bedroom to celebrate the beginning of our new life.

Much later, Jason got up, called the attorney and made all the arrangements for receiving his inheritance. We would have to travel into the city so that he could sign some papers and transfer the money to his, actually soon to be OUR, account. Hence, the next week was a flurry of activity.

First we went to the attorney to make sure this landfall was real. We both knew that the money was actually a gift from our "higher support team" so we could complete our mission. It was not that somehow they made Jason's uncle die, but rather that they invisibly shifted us to a parallel reality in which this money came into our life.

Actually, the money had been trying to come into our life for over six months, as that was the original date on the letter. We had changed so much in those six months that it was a good thing that we did not get that money before now. Who knows if we would have been able to handle it an appropriate manner then?

Now, our heads were clear, so we consulted our higher guidance as to how to best manage our new money. First we would go to the attorney, and then we would find a good company to manage it. Managed correctly, this amount of money could take care of us for many years. That is, if we even needed it after we returned to Gaia's core.

All of the business of re-setting our lives took about two months. In that time we also planned our simple wedding, which we would have in our cabin with our neighborhood friends. Yes, we did buy the cabin, which was always our dream. We told everyone that we were going on a year honeymoon, which in fact was true.

One of our best friends would live in the cabin and take care of it for us. He loved to garden, so he would keep up our backyard garden. Everything was falling into place. Jason and I knew that all of this occurred because of our friends in, literally, "higher places." We stepped up our meditation, as we knew that the temptations of our new life could tempt us to forget our mission.

Our higher dimensional team was with us every day in our meditations. Mytre and

Mytria communicated with us on a regular basis, as did Mytrian and the Arcturian. It was very clear to me that the day that the Arcturian came into my kitchen was the beginning of my/our new life. The next new beginning in *our* life was our marriage, which I now share.

Our friends made us spend the night before our wedding in a nearby hotel room. None of them had much money for gifts, so they decided to work together to decorate the cabin for our wedding. One of them had a local friend who could legally marry us and arranged for her to come to our cabin.

We decided to be completely ready for our yearlong "honeymoon" before our wedding, so everything was planned by the end of our two-month period of creating our new life. Finally, everything was ready, and we were staying at the hotel while our friends decorated our cabin. They were all very creative, so we knew they would do a wonderful job.

Now we could have afforded a fancy hotel further down the mountain, but we loved the life we had created here and did not want to change it. We had started several trusts for ecological foundations for the animals, forests, atmosphere, oceans, etc. We did not know what would occur in the core of Gaia, except we knew that Jason and I would *always* be together.

We also made a will leaving the money to our friends. Neither one of us had any family, so we divided the money equally among our friends. Jason even put the money in OUR name before we were married. He told me, "We are ONE person. Everything is to be in OUR name." I was so happy that I had to keep pinching myself to see if it was all a dream.

"All physical life is a *dream*," reminded the Arcturian in one of our meditations. Jason and I reminded each other of this message as we snuggled into bed in our pre-marital motel room. We had had our pre-marital dinner in the local tavern, walked back to our room and fallen into bed laughing from a bit too much beer.

"Can we consummate our marriage before we get married?" Jason asked with a glint in his eyes. I answered him with a long kiss.

The next morning we woke very early. We took a walk along the trail running past the motel, had breakfast at the same tavern and went back to our room to get ready for our wedding. We knew the bride and groom were supposed to be apart before the wedding, but we did not want to ever be apart.

We had our wedding clothes with us, so at the appointed time we donned our wedding clothes and drove to our cabin to become husband and wife. I was so happy that I felt as though I would burst. Fortunately, I could see that Jason was just as excited.

When we came around the final curve to our cabin we saw our friends lined up in front of our door. They were all dressed in their "Sunday-best" with bright smiles on their faces. They formed two lines of people, which we were guided to walk between.

When we got to the front door, our Best Man opened it and the Maid of Honor guided us through the amazingly decorated house and out the back door. They had planned the wedding in the exact spot where we had first been taken up in the Spaceship.

"When we saw that, Jason and I both burst out in tears. How could we leave these amazing friends? What if we never saw them again? "Live in the NOW!" we both heard the Arcturian inside our consciousness.

Since this was the most wonderful NOW we could imagine, we both smiled as we were guided to the lovely woman who would marry us. We had totally trusted our friends, and they had created the most perfect wedding possible. The ceremony was beautiful, the food was delicious, the conversations were filled with joy and laughter and the hugs were abundant.

Finally, it was time to sneak into our bedroom and get our travel clothes on. We had already fully packed the van we bought for our trip, as we would leave the car for our friend who was living in the cabin.

We now had the money to have an elaborate, expensive wedding, but this was the most perfect wedding we could imagine, and it was FREE. Everything was part of our gift from our friends. They had all cooked food, decorated the cabin and shared their most important gift of love and laughter.

When we came out of our room dressed in our travel clothes, we hugged them all. Our laughter turned to tears. Everyone, even the woman who had married us and become our instant friend, was crying.

Once Jason had driven out of their vision, he pulled our car over so that we could hug and cry, from happiness and a bit of sorrow. Then, we drove down the mountain and into the unknown. We did not know if we would ever see our dear friends again, but we knew we would carry them, and this day, in our hearts forever.

As we drove down the mountain, we knew that our old life had ended, and we were beginning a new one.

Back From Lemuria Part 2

Arcturian Campsite Message

JASON SPEAKS:

Somewhere in the midst of all that Sandy has told you, we also planned the route for our great adventure. We decided to camp as often as possible so that we could be closer to Mother Nature. We were too excited to camp at what we had determined as our first camp, so we drove all night and started our adventure at our second campsite.

We arrived there early in the morning, chose our site, crawled back to sleeping area at the back of our new van and instantly fell asleep. The Camp Ranger who wanted our registration and payment for the site awakened us in just a few hours. We were still so excited that we could not go back to sleep and began setting up our site.

We had discussed that we would stay at this site for a few days to relax after all the excitement of the last two months. However, we did not expect the emotions that arose as soon as we had stopped our busy activity and realized the massive responsibility of our mission

We both felt in a moment of transition in which we were terrified, excited, relieved, sad and jubilant. Because our emotions were so diverse and intense, we could not settle into happy. We had brief moments of happiness, but then our confused thinking came in to disrupt that peaceful moment.

All our lives we had been seeking, searching, healing and working. Hence, we did not know how to create and accept a life that was NOT based on "working hard to achieve." Of course we had had our wonderful adventures beyond time, but we did not create that life.

We totally changed our lives once we first came to our cabin, but we still had to work. Now the financial support for our mission had easily entered our life, but we had no idea as to how to start. After our tent was pitched and our site totally set up for our stay, the doubt and confusion overtook us and we entered the tent to "take a nap." Instead, we both went into a deep trance and actually saw the Arcturian in the small tent with us. The Arcturian was in Its primary form of a cloud-like being with flickering stars, but Its usual size was condensed to fit into the tent. Our trance deepened further as the Arcturian spoke to us.

"Did you forget that we have been assisting you for your entire life? We see that you are both at the biggest crossroads of your lives. Therefore, you are about to LET GO of your ego! Your ego is not a 'bad thing,' as there are no bad or good things in the reality that you are NOW creating.

"There is only life—the life YOU have created. You have created a wonderful life for yourselves, and now you are prepared to fulfill your mission of communing with all life. In order for you to commune with all life, beginning with the elements and elementals, you need to gain mastery over your energy fields.

"As you are now aware, you are both physical expressions of Mytre and Mytria who ascended into fifth-dimensional consciousness long before your present timeline. However, when you are involved in achieving, trying, working and creating you can forget that you are already Masters of your energy field in the higher expression of your Multidimensional SELF.

"Once you remember that YOU are *also* Ascended Masters on a higher frequency of your Multidimensional SELF, you perceive your physical vehicle as a link to the third dimensional reality you are serving. We say 'serving' because your Ascended Master SELF no longer needs to take an earth vessel for experience.

"You only take an earth vessel for service to the planet on which you have taken that form. As an Ascended Masters you no longer need an earthen vessel to evolve, learn or expand your consciousness. Your evolution, learning and expansion no longer occur in the third/fourth dimension, but in the fifth dimension and beyond.

"During this process, the earth vessel that your ascended SELF is wearing can become confused. You see, in a reality in which you have moved into your initiations for ascension, you generally really enjoy your physical life. Of course, the Piscean Age is filled with stories of the great suffering of the ascended ones, but that is only because of the level of perceptions of those who observed their Master's ascension.

"For one thing, the Piscean Age was about 'worshiping' the higher forces. Since the Kali Yuga, the last 2,000 years of the Grand Cycle has been the furthest from the light, as it is focused primarily on the dark. It is the cycle in which the polarities are the most extreme and the Truth is the most distorted.

"Fortunately, you are now in the Golden Age in which entire societies, and in your case the entire planet can ascend beyond the illusions of polarity. Free of the illusion of polarity, you can remember how to perceive what is *in between* what you had formerly observed as opposites. In this manner, the ascending ones can find that center place of peace and unconditional love and choose to live within that center.

"Since entrance into the Golden Age has just occurred within your illusion of *time*, your human ego is still accustomed to being at the helm of your life. In order for your higher expressions of SELF to replace your ego as Captain of your earth vessel, you must unconditionally love your ego, unconditionally forgive your ego and unconditionally accept your ego.

"Unconditional acceptance can be perplexing, as it is a new concept. For most of your incarnations within the last 2,000 years, you had to become 'better' because you were never 'good enough.' This logic already seems flawed to your expanding consciousness, but do you remember how important it was to be 'better' before you awakened?"

"I know that both Sandy and I had thought of our selves in that manner. Our transition from 'not being good enough' to 'loving ourselves unconditionally' occurred during the time we spent with our own higher expressions of SELF.

"Yes," continued the Arcturian, "And now your world is on the cusp of meaning no 'time.' For more earthly lives than you could count, *now* meant it was 'time to do something.' Hence, the shift into NOW meaning 'no time' is very novel to the third dimensional memory of your myriad incarnations before this Golden Age.

"In your other incarnations on Earth, *now* meant that *something* should be *done*. This cognitive shift from now meaning *you have to do it now*, to NOW being the *no time* of the fifth dimension and beyond can be difficult. Hence, all they have to DO in order to ascend can overwhelm our brave inhabitants of ascending Earth.

"In fact, the main *action* of 'doing' is transmuting into the *knowing* of 'being.' Through your physical incarnations on third/fourth dimensional Earth you had to use your muscles, your labor, your concentration and actions to create something in your reality.

"Within your NOW, which is on cusp of transmuting into the fifth dimension, it is NOT the *doing* of your physical body that creates your world, but the frequency of your *being*. The frequency of your being is determined by the state of your consciousness.

"Hence, you are beginning to realize that *your state of consciousness determines your actions*. If you are attuned to a higher state of consciousness, your actions flow in a creative fashion. On the hand, when you are in a lower state of consciousness, your actions meet a great deal of resistance, and you feel like you are 'working too hard.'

"To maintain a higher state of consciousness, your thoughts and emotions needs to be in alignment with each other. But, there is yet another factor. The *frequency* in which your thoughts and emotions are alignment is vital. If your thoughts are of the higher frequency of striving to remain in connection with your SELF, but your emotions are stuck in some EGO version of fear, your attention will be "separated" in two different directions.

"If your emotions are loved-based, but your thoughts are fearful, you will be pushing the accelerator with one foot while your other foot is on the breaks. Many of our ascending ones have found themselves in this situation. Do you remember that when you were first learning a difficult task you could not talk while doing it? You could only *do* the new task. If you added talking, your concentration was disrupted and you could not effectively continue the new task.

"You are now being asked to live your daily life in the same reality that you have known for your entire life while you, simultaneously, enter a frequency of reality that has a completely different operating system. What would happen to your computer if you kept your old operating system running while you also ran a new, totally different, operating system?

"Your computer would become so confused that it would likely *crash*. We see that many of ascending ones are feeling as though they will *crash*. In fact, you all will crash and are crashing on a continual basis, which is why your thoughts are both illumined and confusing while your emotions run from joy to fear.

"You are in the process of shifting from the operating system of your third dimensional brain into the operating system of your multidimensional mind. Therefore, both brain and mind are in great transition. During this transition you will have brief moments in which these two brains are in alignment.

Within that moment your multidimensional mind can connect through your third dimensional brain to create feelings of euphoria and higher creative thoughts.

"It is these moments of temporary connection that you get a glimpse of the new life of the new you. Your challenge is when your two operating systems fall out of alignment and you 'crash.' When this occurs, remember to commend yourself for your temporary alignment rather than chastising yourself for falling out of alignment.

"When you do temporarily fall out of alignment with your true SELF, remember that 'practice makes perfect.' Then, send your 3D self extra unconditional love and unconditional forgiveness for temporarily falling out of alignment. Also, give your self some unconditional acceptance. You volunteered to participate in the immense process of personal and planetary ascension.

"Remember that it was the Ascended Master, you, who volunteered to assist dear planet Gaia, upon whose body you have worn different earth vessels during myriad physical incarnations. There are also Ascended Ones who are new to Gaia. They have come to Earth NOW because it is their special service to aid all life forms to ascend back to their higher expressions of SELF.

"Whether it is your first incarnation on Earth or one of your many earthly incarnations, you have volunteered to assist with the vast endeavor of releasing the shackles of the habit of being only physical.

"Whether our volunteers are new to this experience or have lived it for decades, they are all together in the NOW of the ONE. Therefore, we ask that you look into your life with the eyes of unconditional love to see those who have also volunteered to assist Gaia with Her transition."

When the Arcturian completed Its message, the temperature inside the tent was so hot that we rushed out of it and bumped into our Lemurian friend, Lantern. How wonderful. Lantern was to be our guide on our great adventure of communing with all life.

Suzanne Lie, Ph.D.

Back From Lemuria Part 3

Communicating with Ether and Earth

JASON CONTINUTES:

At first we did not know it was Lantern we had bumped into, and I do mean that Sandy and I both knocked into him together. We were so dazed by the Arcturian's message, or maybe we were only partially physical, that we ran into a tall, slim man who was standing right in front of our tent.

It was not until Lantern spoke to us telepathically, that we realized who it was. Somehow, we recognized his telepathic voice, but maybe it was his signature frequency that was familiar. Either way, we were graced with the joyous and loving laughter that Lantern releases into Gaia's planet. I remember how his laughter could be heard even above the huge crowd at the Lemurian Celebration.

"We wondered where you were hiding," teased Sandy.

"It appears to me that you and Jason are the ones who have been hiding. Was it too crowded in the tent with the Arcturian?" Lantern laughed. "Your faces are white. You are not aware that the great heat in the tent was because your Lightbodies burst forth while the Arcturian spoke. I had to place a holo-picture around your tent so others in the camp would not be shocked."

"Our Lightbodies burst forth?" we spoke as one person.

Lantern just laughed and said, "Put on your hiking gear," as he manifested two backpacks in front of us. "We are going for a hike!"

"But we only slept for a few hours, and we need to eat," complained Sandy.

"Oh, we can do all of that on the trail," said Lantern as he pushed us back in the tent and loaded the backpacks in the van.

"I have paid for this site for a week. We will leave the van at the ranger station at the base of our trail. Now, hurry up, we need to be up the mountain a bit before it gets dark."

Sandy and I were shocked by Lantern's attitude. He was still his jovial self, but we had never known him to be so authoritative.

"It is the NOW!" he responded to our thoughts.

That sentence got our attention more than anything else. We quickly changed, grabbed some trail food for our packs and got into our van. Lantern told me where to park the van and went in to pay at the ranger station.

"How did he get money for the site and the parking?" Sandy asked as Lantern walked toward the ranger station.

I smiled in response and told her I would ask him.

"Ask me what?" said Lantern with a twinkle in his eye.

"Uh, where did you get your money?"

"Oh, I got it from the same place that I got your back packs. I manifested it," he said as he led us up to the trailhead.

Nothing else was said for hours. Sandy's and my Lightbody *must* have been activated as we did not get tired and were never hungry, at least until evening. However, as the Sun began to set, we both became extremely hungry and tired. Sandy was the first to speak up.

"Lantern, do you think we are close to our campsite?" she asked, trying to keep the fatigue out of her voice.

"Would you like to rest?"

"No, no. I am fine. I was just wondering how much further we had to go."

"Further is a third dimensional concept," Lantern returned.

"I know I am more Lightbody than before, but my encasement is still very physical," Sandy said.

"Is that what you believe?"

"Wow," we both exclaimed. I had let Sandy appear to be the only one who was tired, but I was also about to fall over. "Is our belief making us tired?" I said trying not to sound rude.

"Yes, of course. Your Lightbody has no fatigue at all, as it has not even moved."

We were really surprised by that statement until the light went on in Sandy's head and she exclaimed, "Our Lightbody is fifth dimensional so it resonates beyond time!!"

"But only if we believe it," I continued.

Lantern said nothing else, but turned and continued up an especially steep part of the trail.

"It is getting dark now. We need to see the trail when it's so steep," we both complained.

"You will ask the Great Mother to guide you," Lantern projected into our hearts.

"Did you feel that?" Sandy asked me. "It felt like he spoke directly into our hearts."

"I did that because you will need to open your hearts to follow the Mother when you cannot see."

As the Sun dropped below the horizon, the trail became dark with many shadows and illusions.

"Hmm," said Lantern, "This looks like the lower Astral Plane. You'd best be careful."

"Are you trying to scare us?" I said.

"Oh no. I am trying to warn you. Remember that the Arcturian activated your Lightbody. Therefore, you are fully awake to the dark ethers of the Lower Astral Plane. It appears that Gaia is asking us to communicate with the wounded 'ethers' of Her planet."

"Yes, we are indeed in the Lower Astral plane," Sandy whispered. "Do you think this is on purpose to make us use our Lightbody to navigate our way?"

"Yes, of course," I said. "I keep forgetting that many Lemurians are members of Indian Nation. They teach by experience, which allows each person to learn in their own way."

Our conversation had to cease, as we had to focus in order to navigate the steep, dark trails while being confronted by dark images flying through the ethers. Finally, we came over a rocky hill and saw what appeared to be demons rushing towards us.

"What should we do?" we asked Lantern with fear in our voice.

"You are here to communicate with the beings of the ethers," was all he said. However, it was just enough, as it reminded Sandy and I to stand firm and send unconditional love to the dark illusions.

"Good," guided Lantern. "Attention amplifies that to which you attend. When you are non-reactive to the dark images, you diminish them by withdrawing your attention. When you are ready, remember that they can be healed by your unconditional love."

We knew that these images could not harm us. In fact, when we viewed them through our unconditional love we could see that they wanted our help. We released all thinking and felt the unconditional love that the Arcturian had just shared with us. Once we felt that unconditional love inside of our selves, we could share it with the dark ethers of the lower fourth dimension.

As we stood firm and focused on unconditional love, we could feel our Lightbodies expanding out from our spine. We observed as our inner light intertwined with our unconditional love to transmute the fearful images into sparkles of light.

This light flowed into love as the ethers around us cleared more and more. By the time the moon was up, everything around us glistened and sparkled. Even the clouds that covered the sky all day cleared to reveal a sparkling universe above us.

Lantern stood beside us and pointed out the many stars that had planets that we had visited in our higher expressions of Mytre and Mytria.

"Do you remember how Mytre and Mytria bonded with the Mother of their Pleiadian planet?" asked Lantern.

"Yes, we do," said Sandy speaking for both of us.

"To communicate and merge with the elements and elementals you will need to listen closely to your transmuting earth body, as well as your higher expressions of Mytre and Mytria. You have perceived your earth vessels as YOU and Mytre and Mytria as separate and *outside* of you.

"To complete your task you will need to feel your higher expressions of SELF *inside* of you, while you also perceive your earth vessel as ONE with Gaia's Earth.

"The path of ascension is not outside of you, but within your body, which is a component of Gaia's body. Do you understand what I am saying?" concluded Lantern.

"Yes," I said. I looked at Sandy and she was shaking her head yes. "But I think that this change in perception will be more difficult than we think," she whispered under her breath.

Through The Portal

Lantern merely smiled and started back up the trail. However, Sandy and I became lost in our thoughts and forgot to listen to the earth element. Sandy started to slip, and I lost my balance when I tried to catch her. Before we knew it we were sliding down the trail towards a sheer cliff. Lantern did not try to help us, which made me angry, so angry that my consciousness dropped, and I started to feel fear.

I was becoming confused and disoriented when I heard Sandy yell my name. She had grabbed onto a tree and was putting out her hand to me. I reached out and grabbed it, but it dislodged her hold on the tree and we both began to fall.

"We must call the earth elementals," yelled Sandy.

When we both called to Gaia's earth elementals to stop our fall, we suddenly became very calm. Suddenly, our fall was occurring in slow motion. Therefore, we both saw an opportunity to direct ourselves towards a large bolder. As our world became increasingly slow motion we realized that we were leaving 3D time.

We focused *not* on our fall, but on the huge rock and the firm soil beneath us. In a flash of *no time*, we were snuggled up to the bolder with Gaia's warm dirt on every inch of our bodies. All we could do was laugh and say thank you, thank you, thank you to Gaia's earth elementals.

Back from Lemuria Part 4

Communicating With Sylphs and Undines

LANTERN SPEAKS:

Jason and Sandy were so bruised and exhausted from their fall that I led them to a nearby flat area and helped them pitch their small tent. Once done, they crawled inside with their sleeping bags, got into them, dirt and all, and instantly fell asleep. At least they thought they were "just" sleeping. Actually, they were beamed up to the Ship to be taken to the Restoration Chamber where their injuries were healed.

When they woke up just after Sunrise, they were still covered with dirt, but healed of all wounds. They were in shock when they climbed into the tent, so they did not realize how badly they were injured.

When they emerged from their tent, I had made some hot coffee and some warm camp food. After saying good morning, we ate in silence and enjoyed the hot coffee. The fog was so thick that we could hardly see each other, but we could converse. Jason and Sandy began comparing the vivid dreams they had had and figured out that they had gone to the Ship.

"I could only remember one room though," said Sandy, "and I think I was sleeping there. NO! I was healing."

"Yes," answered Jason. "I think we were in the Restoration Room. No wonder we feel so much better than last night. I was afraid that we were really hurt, but we were going into shock and could not really feel our injuries. Did we go on the ship?"

"Yes," I replied. "We did not want your mission to be cut short, but you could not have continued up the mountain without your healing."

"How come I cannot remember very much?" asked Sandy.

"It is common that people who are injured and go to the Restoration Room do not remember. Also, since your Lightbodies were already activated, they greatly accelerated your healing process. In fact, much of your healing was done by your own Lightbodies."

"Our Lightbody can heal us?" they both asked.

"It is more as if your Lightbody was never wounded. It is of a higher resonance than the physical plane, so nothing third dimensional can harm it. But, as Sandy said before, your earth vessel still surrounds your

Lightbody, and it was your physical form that needed the healing.

"How are you feeling now?"

"Confused," said Sandy and Jason agreed.

"How come they did not take the dirt off us when we were in the Restoration Room?" asked Jason.

"You may be surprised, but you made such a deep connection with the earth elementals that they wanted to remain with you until you were fully recovered," I answered.

"Maybe that explains the strange dreams I was having last night," said Sandy. "I kept seeing these little beings around me that looked like gnomes. They were very busy doing some kind of work. I felt like I was a young child having one of my many dreams in which I visited the Land of Faerie."

"I had similar dreams," said Jason. "I saw myself when I was a small boy and loved to play in the mud and create small villages. Sometimes the villages would dry in the Sun and stay together for a day or two; that is if I could keep my dog away. I also remember that we had foggy mornings like this, which I always loved.

"My dog and I would take long walks in the fog, and my dog would always find our way back home. I have not thought of any of my childhood in years. I remember now that I talked to the trees, animals, the clouds and any 'imaginary' being that I believed were real."

"It is interesting how we are talking about our childhood. Do you think that is because we have talked with the earth and ether elementals?" asked Sandy. "Maybe we did that when we were children and forgot. I remember when I was young I also talked to birds, dolls, plants and even bugs. I knew everything was alive. When I got older, I thought that was a ridiculous thought. Now I know that my child was right."

All three of us laughed and continued to chat as we cleaned up the area. "There is a lovely lake just up the hill a bit further. You can clean yourselves there. However, you will need to commune with the air and water elementals to see through this fog," I said preparing them for their next challenge.

SANDY SPEAKS:

I could hear through Lantern's jovial message that he was preparing us for our next challenge. Fortunately the trail ahead was not too steep, as we could not see very far ahead of us. I could tell that Jason was a bit concerned and felt very protective of me. I gathered from Lantern's earlier message that we were more injured than we thought. We are so blessed to have our galactic friends.

I was just getting ready to put on my pack when Jason came over and gave me a long hug. "I feel like last night was my fault. I am so sorry. We could have been very badly hurt."

"Maybe we were," I said, "but we are healed now. I am going to try to tune into my Lightbody more. I can feel this warm sensation inside that is very different from anything I have ever experienced.'

"I have been having the same sensation. I wonder what will happen," pondered Jason.

As Jason was just getting his pack on, I kissed him and re-assured him that our fall was NOT his fault. "We are in this together," I said as I kissed him one more time. "Now, let's get out of this fog and into that lake."

The short hike to the lake was not easy at all. The "easy" path had a shear drop on one side, so we had to really pay attention to what the earth elementals were telling us about the trail. I am happy they were with me because I quickly became fatigued and my body still hurt all over from our fall. I was wondering how badly we were really hurt when a flashback of our fall came into my mind. I was so surprised that I started to lose my balance.

Then something happened I could not understand. It was as if an invisible hand pulled me back into balance. Once I was centered back inside of me I heard Lantern laugh as he said, "Remember that YOU extend far beyond your physical self."

Jason softly said, "What was he talking about?"

"I will tell you later. Remind me would you, as my 3D memory is very sporadic."

This time I heard Jason's laughter as he said, "Yeah, mine too," which made me laugh as well. As if our laughter had cleared our way, we turned the next switchback to see a gently sloping hill leading to a magnificent lake.

Jason and I literally ran up the hill, dropped our packs, shed our filthy clothes and jumped into the lake. In the distance we heard Lantern's comforting laughter. When I felt the clear water of the lake caress my body, I began to feel what I thought were fish gently rubbing next to my legs.

At first it was a bit disconcerting, but then I surrendered into the feeling and remembered that I was in their home. I so loved the feeling of the water that I dove down and opened my eyes to see that there were NO fish. However, there were wonderful, gossamer beings flowing through the water.

"Hello dear human one," I heard in my consciousness, "We are the Undines. We are the fifth-dimensional water elementals."

I became so hypnotized by their presence that I lost all track of where I was or how far I had swum. When I came to the surface again, I was disoriented and could not see Jason or Lantern anywhere. I was a good swimmer, so I was not frightened, but I did know that I had to head back to where I jumped into the lake.

"Follow us," I heard the whispering voices again. I went under water to see them waving for me to follow. Could I trust them? I could only see them when I was under water, but then I couldn't see the shoreline. I decided to flip over on my back and look up into what had become a clear blue sky filled with wispy clouds.

I was just thinking that the flowing and wispy nature of the clouds reminded me of the Sylphs when I heard, "Hello Human one. We are the Sylphs. We are the fifth dimensional air elementals. We want you to know that you can trust our Undine friends. Also, we will part our clouds to show you the way to your human friends."

Then, the most miraculous thing happened. The clouds seemed to part in a manner that they pointed to a certain location on the distant shore. How could I have swum so far? I was not sure if I could make it back there, as I had been swimming for a long time.

"Do not worry," I heard the Undines and Sylphs speaking into my heart. "We have told your friends where you are."

I had no recourse but to trust them, so I followed the *cloud path* of the Sylphs while my head was above water and the Undines when my head was under water. It seemed that the elementals were giving me energy, or was it love? Maybe energy and love are the same?

I was so absorbed in my own thoughts that I did not hear or see the small boat coming toward me until I heard Jason calling my name. Jason's voice pulled me out of my reverie. When I saw the boat I was so excited that I took a gulp of water and involuntarily went under water. Instantly, my Undine friends surrounded me, and just a short distance away, I saw another group of Undines guiding Jason.

I never knew Jason could swim so fast, but he was with me in seconds and pulled me to the surface. Lantern reached over from his small boat and helped me aboard, and Jason climbed into the other side. When I settled down I asked Lantern, "Where did you get the boat?"

With his bright smile and kin laugh he said, "I manifested it."

Later that evening when we were sitting by a warm campfire sipping tea, Jason said, "I thought we were going to help the elementals, but it turned out that they have helped us."

We held each other tight and looked out across the glorious scene of stars reflecting on the still lake. In that NOW we KNEW that *we were not alone* and ONE with Gaia forever!

Suzanne Lie, Ph.D.

Pleiadian Perspective on Ascension Book 5
Through The Portal
TRANSMUTATION OF LIFE

Through The Portal

Transmutation of Life Part 1

Living In-Between

JASON SPEAKS:

The next morning we awoke to a gorgeous day. Lantern had let us sleep in, as he knew we needed it. Sandy and I had thought we were going on a year- long vacation and gradually getting to know the elementals so that we could help them. However, it turned out that we were on a crash course in which we were the ones asking for help.

All along we had only considered that we could get assistance from the Galactics in the higher dimensions. On this trip up the mountain we discovered that the planet itself was our best friend. For many generations we were taught that the planet was a place to plunder and do with as we pleased.

We were taught that humanity was the master of our world. However, even the smallest bird would not spoil its nest, whereas humanity has repeatedly placed their entire planet to the verge of destruction. Gaia needed to leave the third dimensional frequency because it was becoming increasingly difficult for Her to keep Her planet habitable.

Since our encounters with and assistance from the elementals of ether, earth, air and water, Sandy and I would never look at our world in the same way. I am forever grateful to the air and water elementals, the Sylphs and Undine, for leading me to Sandy.

I was sure that Lantern could have helped me, and he did manifest a boat to rescue her. However, I did not even imagine that Sandy was in trouble. I thought she was basking on some warm rock like Mytria and Mytre loved to do.

Then, right when I was starting to get concerned, I felt a message enter my consciousness. I tuned into Sandy's signature frequency and realized that she was becoming increasingly frightened about something. I had the feeling that I should look up into the sky, and I saw a parting in the clouds. I instinctively knew that I should follow that path.

I was just thinking how far away the end of the cloud path was when I heard Lantern call me from the water's edge. I watched as he manifested a small rowboat, which I ran toward and we both jumped into it.

"Follow the trail in the sky," I said to Lantern. Once we were in the water, the

Undines also created a trail in the water to follow. As soon as I saw Sandy, I jumped into the lake to meet her.

When we got back to the shore by our camping site, Sandy and I hugged each other and thanked the elemental again! After a wonderful evening and night by the lake, we went back into our tent and instantly fell asleep.

The next morning I received an Arcturian message while I was semi-awake. I was in a state of consciousness *in-between* being awake and asleep when I received a direct communication from the Arcturian. When I almost woke up, I lost connection with the message, so I surrendered back into direct communication, and I almost fell asleep.

When I fully awoke, I quietly got my notebook and pen that I always carry and left the tent to try to receive the message by writing. I have found that if I, or Sandy, do not write or type the message while I am receiving it, I will forget most of it.

I closed my eyes and focused inside to return to that "in-between" place. When I felt myself in that state of consciousness, I placed the pen on the paper so that I could *take dictation*.

"Our Dearest One," began the Arcturian message, the in-between frequency of consciousness that you are experiencing is becoming your primary state of resonance. You still hold a physical form, but the connection to your Multidimensional SELF and multidimensional consciousness is becoming more and more secure.

"You have successfully held that frequency for all of your encounters with your higher expressions of SELF. We, the Arcturians, are now teaching you *not* to become attached to *just* the messages but, also, to that frequency of consciousness you are in when you receive that message.

"In other words, we are here to assist you to raise your baseline frequency from the third-dimensional frequency that you have known during your physical incarnations to the *new* baseline frequency of ascending Gaia. The message we sent you in the tent was about calibrating your primary attention to this new baseline frequency.

"While resonating to this new baseline consciousness, you can more easily communicate with us on a regular basis. Now that you have returned from the realms of sleep, but before you have experienced any 3D stressors, we ask you return to that in-between frequency. In this state of consciousness it is easier for you to 'take dictation,' as we repeat our former message. Please adjust your consciousness NOW."

I closed my eyes to shut out the physical world around me and took a long breath. I found that I easily slipped into that in-between state, because everyone else was still asleep. The early morning has always been my favorite time of the day as I could be in both worlds, at least while my eyes were closed.

However, once I opened my eyes, my attention turned *out* to the 3D world rather than *in* to the higher worlds. For that reason, I wrote the Arcturian message with my eyes half-closed. I imagined that I was lying in the tent again to fool my consciousness into thinking that I was in that same semi-awake state.

It was then that I remembered a mediation I had a few days before in which I saw/felt an Arcturian face directly in from of my Third Eye. At first I only saw/felt a sparking light take on a vaguely human face with a swirling third eye. I was riveted and looked directly into the Arcturian face until I felt a deep connection between us.

The first time this happened, and again now, I could feel a direct download from the Arcturian's face into my being. This feeling rushed throughout my entire body, which became very hot and tingly. The tingles felt almost as though the atoms of my body were expanding, and I was floating outside of my body while still remaining inside my form.

It then became very clear that I was no longer limited to my human form. For a brief moment I felt the Arcturian ME as my primary SELF. When I felt my consciousness begin to lower I looked back at the face to get another blast of the Arcturian energy.

As I wrote down that past experience, which I had totally forgotten, I realized that I was being trained to realize that I had entered a new frequency of consciousness. I remembered that I had often visited that frequency while in meditation, but now I was being guided to *always* live within this next octave of resonance.

My challenge was to remain in that frequency of consciousness with my eyes open. Once my eyes opened, I saw all the "habit markers" that made me fixate *only* on the physical world. In fact, even writing my experience was turning my attention outwards.

Through The Portal

I took a long breath to relax into the state of consciousness that I was in when I was just waking up and beginning to receive the Arcturian's message. But I was having difficulty remembering how that frequency of consciousness felt and opened my eyes in frustration.

Instantly, my consciousness lowered into my 3D operating system. I quickly closed my eyes again and visualized the Arcturian face before me. Another flow of higher energy entered me, and I was able to continue with this type of "dictation."

I then received that I was being trained to receive and document inter-dimensional messages while maintaining a higher frequency of baseline consciousness. While resonating to this "in-between" consciousness I could be in both worlds at once.

Therefore, I could receive information that was far beyond my physical brain's capacity to understand. I took another long breath to recalibrate to this higher frequency of consciousness and could feel my multidimensional mind above my physical brain sending down streaks of light to connect with my third dimensional thinking.

I had to stop writing a moment to experience the novel experience of consciously getting information from my multidimensional mind. It felt as if there was a multidimensional library above my physical head to which I was becoming increasingly connected. I realized that when this connection was complete, I would be able to simultaneously experience more than one dimension of reality.

This state of consciousness accessed a higher mental operating system, which was too difficult for my physical brain to remember. While I was in-between my higher self and my physical state, I could connect with my multidimensional mind. Once connected with my multidimensional mind, I could allow the higher information to flow through my physical brain and into my body.

It appeared that my earth vessel was more evolved than my human brain, as my body is an *animal* that is free of ego. My physical brain is connected to my ego because it is ego's *job* to assist me to integrate with humanity. Thus, my ego told me to ignore anything that distracted me from my 3D *work*.

Suddenly, I had a vision of myself on Venus before I took my first physical incarnation during the fall of Atlantis. I took a long moment to enjoy the feeling of my beloved Venusian home. I felt Sanat Kumara around our entire group while he instructed us how to best assist Gaia.

While still on Venus, Sanat Kumara told us that even if Earth survived, it would be too difficult for us to remain connected to our multidimensional minds. As our consciousness steadily fell to the lower resonance of Gaia's wounded Earth, our multidimensional mind would remain with our fifth dimensional resonance.

When I heard that we would likely lose our connection to the portal of our Multidimensional SELF, my resonance dropped back to the third dimension. I focused my attention once again on the Arcturian face before my Third Eye. I was not sure what this *face* would connect me to, but the feeling was wonderful and my consciousness steadily expanded.

I was wondering if I could re-connect me with my multidimensional mind when I began to feel my body, not my brain, connecting to my multidimensional mind, as well as to my Multidimensional SELF. Interestingly, the body that I had maligned for my entire life was leading me back to an expanded connection with my SELF.

While I took long breaths to reconnect with the higher base-line frequency, I was told that I would not have the euphoria this time, so that I could allow this feeling to become "normal." I was happy to hear that because my emotions and sensate body had been on a roller coaster.

In this new, expanded state of consciousness I understood that as my outer world changed more and more each day, I was beginning to *feel a new world within me, rather than around me*. This new world was a frequency inside of me that I was meant to project out into my daily life.

I was to project this energy *out* into my daily life in the same manner as the Arcturian face projected Its energy into me. What if I could feel this way all the time? What if I could live my life in this state of consciousness?

I then realized that if I directly reconnected with the starry face to align my consciousness with this new frequency that the energy of the Arcturian face could answer these questions. It was then that I understood that I had visited this energy/consciousness before.

"Yes, but when your human expression visited this frequency before, it experienced it as a 'roller coaster ride,'" said the Arcturian face. "This *ride* was your human consciousness trying to calibrate to your inner multidimensional consciousness. We are NOW communicating directly with your Multidimensional SELF who has merged with your physical expression in order to assist Gaia.

"Your higher expressions of SELF are among those who volunteered to merge with their third-dimensional expression and slowly expand the range of the energy package that they shared with their incarnated, physical expression. Do you remember how you have felt us, your higher expression, above or before you your entire life?"

I took a moment to preview my life and quickly realized that I had always felt this energy above or around me. However, I never thought of this wonderful feeling as being *within* me.

"You never thought of us as within you because your world taught you that that would be 'conceited' or even 'blasphemous.' We have come to you NOW to assist you to remember that we are *within* you. Furthermore, just as we, your higher expressions of SELF are within you; Gaia's higher expression of New Earth is also within you.

"New Earth is not a place. It is a frequency that you will find inside of your own earth vessel. Actually, your inner connection with your own Multidimensional SELF transports your awareness to New Earth, which is also inside of you. You can only perceive your vast inner reality when YOU take charge of the ego rather than allowing your ego to take charge of you.

"You are very familiar with what we are saying, as lately you have been shifting from the frequency of your ego to the ever-expanding frequency of your Multidimensional SELF many times a day. Is that not correct?'"

"Yes, yes," I said in agreement.

"When you feel your SELF, a calm euphoria fills you. Then, suddenly, something must be DONE in the physical world and your consciousness crashes back into the third/fourth dimension."

"Yes," I agreed again.

"Our *Arcturian face* is not actually a face. It is a *portal* into the higher frequency of your SELF, as well as a portal into our Arcturian Corridor. Within the corridor, which is within you, you feel the consciousness of infinite other beings.

"There is no hierarchical arrangement. Thus, a mosquito is of the same importance as a human king. Every thing and every one is pure energy that has chosen a certain physical form to express their consciousness on third-dimensional Earth.

"From within our corridor, you can more easily perceive that third-dimensional Earth is a holographic projection. This hologram has been experienced as 'real' for so many eons that life has become trapped in that illusion of reality.

"However, the 3D illusions are now collapsing to be revealed as the lowest frequency of a vast spectrum of life on planet Earth. *Earth is not a planet where you go, it is a planet that you ARE.*

"As we close this transmission within your NOW, we wish you to focus on our *face*, which is actually the signature frequency of our Arcturian Corridor. Remember that your life is changing because YOU are changing. The illusions of your physical reality are fading because your consciousness and, thus, your perceptions, are increasingly becoming multidimensional.

"Your ego self is afraid because your human brain cannot compute all that you are experiencing. In other words, you are in the midst of transmuting back to your Multidimensional SELF. That SELF has always been *within* your personal earth vessel in the form of your sleeping Lightbody.

Suzanne Lie, Ph.D.

"As you stand at the entrance of the Corridor, you ARE the Corridor and you ARE your Lightbody returning Home to your true, Multidimensional SELF."

Transmutation of Life Part 2

Kundalini, the Inner Fire

JASON CONTINUES:

My reverie of being in the Arcturian Corridor was interrupted when Lantern said, "I have prepared a quick breakfast before we break camp." Sandy then emerged from the tent and came to give me a morning hug. I stood up, hugged Sandy and we walked the short distance to where Lantern had prepared our simple breakfast.

"You don't need to cook for us," I said.

"You were having an important discussion with the Arcturian and Sandy was just returning from the ship. I didn't want to bother you, but we have a ways to hike today, and I want to get there before nightfall."

"I just got back from the Ship?" asked Sandy with a very excited look on her face. "Why don't I remember that?"

"Your physical body needed to sleep. Also, it was too soon for your human self to remember the information you received," answered Lantern as he gave us our food and some hot tea. Sandy tried to get him to say more, but he refused and went over to take down his tent. Sandy shrugged her shoulders and winked at me. "Do you think you were with me?"

"If I was," I said, "I was talking to the Arcturian. I left the tent so I could write down what I was receiving. I will show it to you later."

Sandy looked disappointed that she couldn't see my message now, but Lantern was rushing us to leave. He was right that we had quite a ways to walk, and the hike was all uphill.

When the Sun was low in the sky, we came around, yet another steep switchback, to reveal the most beautiful green meadow we had ever seen. Sandy and I took off our heavy packs and ran to the meadow to sit, lie and roll in the grass.

"This is like the meadow by our home." I smiled as I looked across the meadow to see what looked like a cabin. "Is that a cabin?" I asked.

"Yes," answered Lantern, "it is our cabin. It's even stocked with canned goods and has a creek and small pond next to it."

Now we were even more excited. We could stay in real cabin with a roof and a bed. We grabbed our backpacks and quickly walked across the meadow and to the door of the cabin.

"Go ahead and open it," said Lantern. "They do not lock cabins up here."

"Did you manifest this?" teased Sandy.

Lantern laughed in reply, "No, but I did rent it. You will need a comfortable place for this next part of your mission. You have not yet interacted with the fire elementals, and this time the fire is inside of you—the fire of your Kundalini."

Sandy and I had no idea how important his statement was or how much it would change our lives forever. In fact, all we could think about was that there was a table and two beds.

We loved being in nature, but we were ready for a few "creature comforts." We claimed the bed in the far corner of the cabin and lay now to relax for just a minute. We woke up hours later to find a fire in the fireplace and the soft light of a kerosene lamp.

"I'm hungry," said Sandy as she walked over to the cabinet to see what canned food we had to choose from. There was a camping stove on a ledge next to the cabinet, which Lantern had already lit to make us some hot tea.

"I am glad you finally woke up," he said as he made the tea. "The moon will be up soon and there is something I want you to see."

Sandy found the can opener and was opening two cans of soup for us all to eat. When Sandy asked Lantern what kind of soup he liked, we realized that Lantern never ate with us. Since he did most of the cooking, we had always assumed that he ate before us.

"You don't eat food do you?" Sandy and I asked at the same time.

"I no longer require food. I am nourished by the forces of light," Lantern responded as he pointed his finger towards the heavens.

"Wow," was our mutual response.

Lantern laughed and said, "Soon you will no longer need to eat."

Before we could ask him our myriad questions, he slipped out the door with the excuse of checking on the Moon. Sandy and I silently sat down at the wooden camping table to eat our soup. What was Lantern up to now?

Just as we were finishing our warm meal, Lantern re-entered the cabin with a bright smile and said, "It is time. Get your coats and come outside."

We excitedly got our coats on and went outside.

"Follow me," said Lantern, which we did.

The full Moon was so bright that we could easily see where we were going. We walked a short distance on a path that led us over a small hill to find another huge meadow. The moon was so bright that we could see every detail in the mystical moonlight.

"It is so beautiful!" gasped Sandy.

"Now close your eyes for a moment and expand your consciousness into a higher frequency," instructed Lantern.

We closed our eyes and took long breaths to expand our consciousness. We knew to keep our eyes closed. "Maintaining that state of consciousness, feel your surroundings with your body," instructed Lantern. "As you do so, allow the physical edges of your body to blur out in all directions.

"Now, tune into the *earth* on which you are standing.

"Feel how the aura of your physical form merges with the earth beneath you.

"Smell the *water* in the air and in the nearby pond.

"Remember the feeling of water on your body as you swam in the lake.

"Allow the soft breeze in the *air* to caress your body." As we did everything that Lantern told us to do, we went into a deep trance and began to feel our bodies in a totally different way. Just when we thought we would float away, Lantern spoke,

"Feel how the *earth* on which you are standing is ONE with your earthen vessel.

"Tune into all the *liquids* in your form as they circulate through your body.

"As you breathe in this soft mountain *air*, feel it within you.

"Feel how the ethers around you are filled with soft moonlight.

"Now, keeping your physical eyes closed, look out through your Third Eye."

I could feel how Sandy was focusing on her Third Eye, just as I was focusing on mine. Instinctively, I reached out and took her hand. Instantly, our consciousness expanded in a burst of light and our Third Eyes blinked open to see a huge light in the sky. As we relaxed into the source of the light, the shape of a huge Starship came into our Third Eye.

We both knew that we could not have seen the Ship with our physical vision, but it was perfectly clear through our Third Eye. When we focused on the Ship, we could feel its multidimensional light and unconditional love streaming into our High Heart.

We allowed the love and light to nest in our High Heart and calmly observed as the light traveled up through the top of our heads and into the soft mountain atmosphere, as well as deep into the core of Gaia's planet.

Instinctively, we followed the light into the now familiar core of Gaia to fully ground our consciousness in the body of Gaia. Now that we were firmly grounded we followed the light traveling up from the planetary core.

As the light rose up from the planetary core, we could feel it slowly rise in frequency. When the light broke through the earth and re-entered our body through our feet, it moved up our legs into the base of our spine.

When the light entered the base of our spine we experienced a great heat move into our human core. The light lingered there until Lantern said, "Are you ready to allow that light to rise up your spine?"

Intuitively we knew that the rising of this light would forever change our lives. We squeezed our hands tighter to give each other support and shook our heads yes. We heard Lantern's voice as if he were within us as he said,

"Feel the *earth elementals* of your body supporting your spinal column.

As you inhale, feel the *air elementals* in your lungs, as well as within every cell of your body.

Imagine the *water elementals* flowing through your blood and bodily fluids.

Now, sense the *fire elementals* from Gaia's Core igniting the fire of your inner Kundalini."

Sandy and I had studied the Kundalini and had had brief experiences of it during meditation and Yoga. However, these experiences only hinted at what we were about to experience.

Fortunately, we remembered to focus on the *earth* and imagine our feet deeply grounded into the earth. We smelled the fresh *air* as it entered our nostrils, and imagined the *waters* of our body calmly flowing to the rhythm of our breath and the beating of our heart.

We realized that we were in the process of activating the *fire* of our Kundalini. We had been prepared for this moment and allowed ourselves to surrender, surrender, surrender as we focused our attention and breath on the base of our spine.

As the multidimensional light entered the base of our spine and activated our Kundalini, our bodies reacted by shaking uncontrollably. Gradually we acclimated to this higher frequency, which allowed the awakened Kundalini to fully merge with our core.

Once the base of our spine was recalibrated to this expanded frequency, the Kundalini began to slowly undulate up and down our spine. Our breathing became louder and more intentional with our out-breath twice as long as our in-breath. In a burst of inner fire, our *root chakra* awakened into a higher frequency of activation.

The inner fire held that space for a moment, as well as for all eternity, before it continued its journey into our *navel chakra*. We felt the light behind our navel as it undulated up and down our spine, allowing us to calibrate then recalibrate again and again to this higher frequency of inner light.

Early emotional images coursed through our minds in a collage of childhood memories, some of which we had completely forgotten. The myriad emotions of these experiences threatened to lower our consciousness, so we focused ONLY on our breath and the sensations in the core of our spine.

Again we shook uncontrollably until we remembered to pull the shaking sensation into our core by surrendering to these new sensations. This inner shaking was almost as if we were shaking *out* parts of our self that could not tolerate this higher light.

We realized that we could best release our old resistance by deeply surrendering to our experience. Once the light stabilized in our second chakra, it began to rise into our *solar-plexus chakra*. By now we had learned how to release the *ashes* of our resistance by breathing into the higher frequency of the rising kundalini.

Slowly, and in a more controlled manner, the kundalini rose up from our navel, through our stomach area and into the many internal organs of our third chakra. We felt each organ as they slowly, or quickly, re-calibrated to this higher frequency of physical resonance. As we surrendered into the expanding frequency of our third chakra, we realized that the concept of eating food would become increasingly unimportant.

Since we were totally in the NOW, we had no thoughts or experience of "time." Slowly and calmly, like a gently breeze, the Kundalini fire entered our *heart chakra*. The journey through our first three chakras was filled with bodily sensations, movements and the constant need to release, release and surrender.

Conversely, the kundalini almost tickled our heart, softly "knocking" at the inner entrance to our heart. We knew that we could open that "door" or return later after we had adjusted to what had already occurred. However, Sandy and I had been fully prepared for this NOW and opened wide the doorway of our heart.

We actually saw the vision of a door opening inwards as we welcomed our own inner fire into our heart. We heard an inner voice saying to us, perhaps warning us, that our lives would be forever changed, but we could always re-enter *time* to adapt when we felt the energies were too challenging. We did not realize the importance of that message.

As we welcomed the light into our heart chakra, we felt an instant sense of bliss that resonated up our backs and into our crown. Again we were tempted to shake, but we remembered to breathe into these novel sensations and accept each one with a slow deep breath. Sometimes we needed to open our mouth and make a loud exhale to remain focused. This action was especially important when the fire entered our *throat chakra*.

In order to unveil the truth hidden in this chakra, we had to take deep inhales and long, slow exhales to release all the lies we had been told and/or said during our many incarnations. We also needed to sing certain sounds and tones to adapt to the new frequencies of inner fire flowing through our vocal cords.

We observed as a beam of blinding light carried the flow of the kundalini over the top of our head and entered our *brow chakra*. This higher light would "blind" us to illusion so that we could focus on *being* the Ascended Master SELF that we saw projected onto our inner mind-screen. As we focused on this inner screen we could sense the kundalini fire as it entered our brow to move deep into our brain.

Like a bride waiting at the altar, we awaited the opening of the portal of our *crown chakra*. As our crown chakra slowly opened, we felt a silent rush of multidimensional light flow into our crown. The entrance of multidimensional light entered our crown and caused the kundalini to repeatedly undulate up and down our spine.

With each undulation our bodies became increasingly filled with bliss and passion for life. This flow of blissful light connected us to the formless light of the ONE as it entered our crown chakra and settled into the third ventricle of our brain, our Sacred

Inner Temple. Within this inner temple, Lord Shiva merged with Lady Shakti in the Sacred Marriage of Spirit (divinity) into Matter (humanity).

For a brief second, out kundalini burst out beyond our spine to blaze its sacred fire out beyond our physical form. This burst of light fully opened our Third Eye then softly returned to our form through our heart chakra to take permanent residence in the Three Fold Flame of our High Heart. Just before we collapsed onto the ground, we felt our High Heart inter-connect with our Third Eye.

The next thing we knew was waking up the next morning in our tiny bed in the cabin. We instantly sat up and simultaneously said, "Was that real, or was it just a dream?"

Across the room we heard Lantern say, "Is there a difference?"

Suzanne Lie, Ph.D.

Transmutation of Life Part 3

Adapting To The Shift

SANDY SPEAKS:

The day after our Kundalini experience we primarily slept, relaxed and played in the nearby pond. It was too cold to stay in the water for very long, but we would lay in the sun, naked, until we were too hot. Then, we would jump in the pond, naked, to cool off. The combination of the very hot and very cold helped us to acclimate to the higher frequency of our body.

Being without any clothing was not an issue, as there was no one else around except Lantern, who also took his clothes off. We felt as though we were playing in the Garden of Eden as we acclimated to wearing a new form. We, of course, were used to "wearing a form," but our body was rapidly being transmuted into a new frequency of form that was completely unique.

One of the reasons why we jumped into the cold stream-fed pond was because the heat of this marvelous sunny day stimulated the Kundalini to flash beyond our body. We could tolerate that feeling for a few minutes, but it quickly became overwhelming. We were not yet accustomed to having our bodies resonate to that frequency.

Lantern explained to us that all the prior experiences of our Higher Self and Lightbody had been through our bi-location. However, now we were not bi-locating. Our actual 3D physical form was gradually being transmuted into Lightbody. Jason and I decided that we would not worry about how that transition would change our entire life.

The process of transmutation of our physical form demanded that we remain in the frequency of the NOW. Hence, we drank the clear water from the creek, *meditated*, lay in the Sun, *meditated*, walked into the meadow, *meditated*, and fell asleep to flow into a very deep *meditation*. Lantern continually reminded us how fortunate we were to be able to dedicate our full attention to this process of transmutation.

We agreed. How could we have worked or driven to the store in this condition? We were very grateful that we could "just" commune with the elementals while we walked, dipped in the water, basked in the sun and looked into the sky. When we sat down by the pond we could clearly see the water elementals, the Undines. We could also commune with them via our High Heart. It was an amazing experience to see their wavering forms flow through the water.

We could feel what the Undines were saying to us. Of course, the elementals did not speak human language. They spoke to us via tones, images and bodily sensations. They also communicated via the sound of water dripping off and traveling over rocks, the slight waves of a strong breeze, the glistening of the sun sparkling off the water's surface and the different aromas of water interacting with our environment.

While we were in the pond, we stayed underwater for as long as we could tolerate the cold in order to feel the water all over our body. It was then that we really began to communicate with the Undines. While water was the only stimuli on every part of our form, we received images, ideas, sensations and something like a voice that we heard inside our heart.

We later learned that this inner voice was how we translated what the elementals were saying to us. At first, we had to totally engulf our full attention on the elemental to establish a deep relationship with its essence.

Hence, we went underwater to connect with the Undines, the water elementals, rolled on the grass, sat on rocks or on the earth to communicate with the Gnomes, earth elementals, and looked up into the sky and focused on the wind or breeze to communicate with the Sylphs, the air elementals.

The most challenging experience was with the fire elementals, the Salamanders, because they communicated through our own Kundalini. Of course, all the elementals of our body *and* our environment exist as ONE interacting and flowing energy field.

However, just as we had to learn the alphabet before we could read, we had to specialize in each elemental separately before we could deeply experience their unity consciousness.

Lantern said that no one had the cabin after us, so we could stay there as long as we needed. Since we were primarily living "out of time," it was good to know that we were free to "dock our earth vessels" here while we re-calibrated them.

I must say, that this experience of total freedom and intimate connection with Mother Nature was divine beyond expression. Jason totally agreed. In fact, we were both so enormously happy and eternally grateful that it was quite easy for us to maintain a higher state of consciousness.

If we were tired, we slept. If we wanted to move we walked or did yoga. If we were hot we got in the water, and sat in the Sun when we got cold. If we were thirsty, which was often due to the rising heat within us, we drank clear mountain water.

The one thing that we forgot about was eating food. Strangely enough though, we began to hear certain plants tell us that they were healthy for our bodies, whereas other said, "Stay away." We also knew that certain roots in the ground would be delicious and different flowers or seeds would be tasty and nutritious.

Lantern encouraged us to pick the plants that called to us and to hold them close to our High Heart to ask our bodies how to prepare them. Sometimes our bodies said, "Eat it now." Sometimes we heard, "Put me in the Sun." or "Put me in the shade." Some said, "I need to be boiled in water" and other plants wanted to be wrapped up and put into the fire.

Because Lantern was there to guide us, we could follow our instincts without the concern that we might be wrong and harm ourselves. Just as plants and foliage from the trees told us what to eat and how to prepare it, the very atmosphere seemed to be whispering sacred information into our hearts.

Since this mountaintop had NO noise from humanity, we only heard the myriad voices of Nature. When we lay back on the big, warm rocks, we could see the Sylphs calling to us from their place in the sky.

"Come with us," they called again and again. Finally we took the invitation and, closing our eyes, we drifted off into a reality in which every being flew, darted, dashed, walked or danced in the ethers of the sky.

Jason and I experienced total joy as we floated on a huge cloud. The cloud was soft and transparent, while it firmly held us in our high, soft platform. As we looked at our world from this perspective, we felt like Angels floating high above the density of our physical world.

While floating on our cloud, we suddenly understood everything about clouds, fog, wind, rain and snow. We don't remember how we learned this information, as it seemed to peacefully enter our consciousness.

From our cloudy viewpoint, we could see how all life had a breath which pulled in new elementals with each inhale. These many elementals intermingled with the bodily elementals to get new information. Some remained within the body while others elementals rushed out into the environment via our exhale.

In this manner, all life interacted with each body, and every body interacted with all life. From our position in the clouds, we could see the many elementals moving into and out of all forms of life. As we looked up into the sky, we saw the Sun shining its multidimensional light down into Gaia and all Her inhabitants.

We returned our full attention to our physical forms and felt the light of the Sun amplify our expanding Kundalini. We decided to share our fire with the Sun by expanding our consciousness from inside the core of our Kundalini and out into the core of the Sun.

Instantly, we were overwhelmed by unfamiliar stimuli, which were hot as a noonday sun, but cool as a soft breeze. As these opposites merged into ONE, we felt our Kundalini flash beyond our body in all directions.

We were free of our physical form and floating into an unknown, but somehow expected, new world. In fact, it was a New Earth. This "new earth" was exactly like our old one, except that we could see many frequencies of expression intertwining like a golden thread in the elaborate tapestry of life.

Through The Portal

Transmutation of Life Part 4

The Beginning

JASON SPEAKS:

When Sandy and I returned to our fifth-dimensional expressions of *unity with all life*, we experienced the feeling of simultaneously flowing back into our forms on the blissful mountain meadow, as well as moving up into the Mothership.

As we entered the Mothership, our energy field immediately transported us into the frequency of the Mothership's Oversoul. Once in that frequency, we merged with our Oversoul SELF.

"Congratulations dear human expressions of our SELF," we heard Mytrian say inside our heart. "You have remembered how to bi-locate."

We took a moment of the NOW to consciously register that statement. Indeed, we were concurrently aware of:

Our Multidimensional SELF resonating to the frequency of our Oversoul

Over-lighting our united Lightbody in the Mothership

Over-lighting our expressions of Mytre and Mytria

Over-lighting our Lightbody SELF on the mountain

Over-lighting our return to the Core of Gaia

All of these versions of our multidimensional reality were occurring within the NOW of the ONE. Finally, we deeply understood the concept of "living in the NOW." We had heard that statement many times, but pushed it to the back of our already overloaded brains. However, NOW we were ONE brain, ONE mind, ONE heart, ONE body and ONE Oversoul.

With this realization, the Arcturian joined us, as did Mytrian, Mytre and Mytria and our Lemurian expression of Lantern. As the ONE multidimensional being, we simultaneously viewed our myriad incarnations in uncountable places, times, planets, galaxies and dimensions.

We remained within the NOW as we remembered that the Oversoul frequency of our SELF had never left the infinity of the ONE. While merged with our Oversoul and beyond, we viewed, and simultaneously lived, the tapestry of our myriad excursions into the worlds of form.

All of these third/fourth dimensional lives sung their tale into our hearts as we lived them in our multidimensional mind. Beyond the *concept* of time, we savored total unity with our Multidimensional SELF.

Gradually, a distant urge came into our awareness. It was the NOW for us to maintain all that we had remembered and bring it back into the Core of our sister Gaia who had taken a planetary form. We were to place this information into Her Planetary Core Crystal and Cornerstone Crystals.

With the recognition of this call, our Oversoul SELF focused on the myriad embodiments we had taken on Earth. Since we NOW resonated beyond time we were able to view, recognize and love our innumerable experiences of form on Gaia's planetary body.

In fact, we unconditionally loved, unconditionally forgave and unconditionally accepted every incarnation we had ever taken on Earth. We felt a great harvest of light and love as each of our incarnations recognized and accepted our gift.

We observed as myriad expressions of our multidimensional light joined us in our Oversoul to be healed from the darkness and confusion of Gaia's polarized reality. Of course none of us actually left the Oversoul. Instead, we bi-located from our Oversoul into the realities of our choice.

Through The Portal

As one being of light, we discussed our myriad incarnations on Earth. We laughed, cried, healed and remembered the vast adventures and challenges of life on a third-dimensional planet ruled by the polarities of light and dark.

Together we merged those polarities, as we remembered all the lessons that living in separation from our SELF had taught us. Finally, it was the NOW for our return to Gaia.

We decided that some of our physical expressions would leave the cycle of earthly incarnation, but some of us would stay on ascending Earth to assist Gaia with Her transmutation.

In a flash of *no time*, our primary focus was in the Core of Gaia. However, NOW *all* our myriad realities on Earth were available to our conscious awareness. We were not surprised when Lantern, Mytre and Mytria, Mytrian and the Arcturian greeted us.

In fact, we could feel all the emanations of our Multidimensional SELF as they resonated back and forth between the Core of Gaia and our Oversoul SELF. We could also feel and perceive all those who had attended the previous Lemurian celebration.

They, too, returned as Lightbodies after their "year" on Gaia's surface. We all recognized each other and shared a wonderful form of lightbody merging, which we somehow knew was the typical form of "lightbody greetings."

Our reverie of merging into Oneness was interrupted when Sanat Kumara came to welcome us back. It was then that we realized that everyone in the group had also connected with their Oversoul to collect the wisdom, power and love from *all* their earthly incarnations.

"Welcome back," resonated Sanat Kumara's voice. Instantly we were all quiet and ready to attend to our next assignment. "Congratulations on your successful mission of communicating with all life. We see that all of you discovered and merged with your Multidimensional SELF.

"I am pleased that you remembered that it is only by living in unity and unconditional love with your planet that you can live in unity and love your Multidimensional SELF. You have also experienced that this degree of unconditional love transmutes you back into your fifth dimensional lightbody.

"Our dear Portal Openers please share what you have learned with others. In fact, we ask you now to share this information with beloved Gaia's Core and Cornerstone Crystals."

In a flash we were transmuted to Gaia's Core Crystal. We circled the Core Crystal and felt the Cornerstone Crystals far behind us in the North, East, South, and West. Our Multidimensional SELF knew that all these crystals regulated Gaia's 'Earth Matrix,' which would need to be transmuted from a third/fourth dimensional matrix into a multidimensional matrix.

Fortunately, all of us had recently experienced our personal transmutation from our third dimensional self back into our Multidimensional SELF. We then heard Sanat Kumara instructing us to turn to our right and share with everyone our personal experiences of transmutation into the fifth dimension and beyond.

We were then told to turn to our left to share our personal experiences again. In this manner, we united our personal experiences into our collective experience. Gaia then joined us in Her somewhat humanoid form to instruct us.

"Greetings my beloved human ones. I ask you now to remember *all* of your collective, multidimensional lessons and experiences of transmutation into Lightbody and wrap them in a bundle of unconditional love.

"My crystals are vast storage chambers for all that has occurred on my planet. There has been such great darkness within the last 2,000 years of my planet that my crystals have become infected with the 'virus' of third dimensional lies and illusions.

"I congratulate you for merging with your fifth, sixth, and seventh dimensional Oversoul SELF. Furthermore, you have merged your personal experiences into your collective experience. I now ask you to share your collective experience with my planetary crystals.

"By sharing the wisdom and power of your experience, as well as the beam of your unconditional love through which you will share it, you will greatly assist my crystals to love, free the lies and illusions, and replace them with the truth that 'it is the NOW' of planetary transmutation.

"Within each crystal, you will perceive a Violet Flame of transmutation. I ask you to send your package of unconditional love directly into the Violet Flame to amplify your story of transmutation of all shadow into light.

"Before we transmute my Core Crystal, we will transmute the four Cornerstone

Crystals. We will begin with the Cornerstone Crystal in the North."

In a flash, we were all transported to the far North, which is the point of the inflow of the multidimensional waves of light that nourish the planet. The crystal was so huge that even though there were many of us, we could stand around it single file.

"I wish you all to remember your many incarnations in my northern territories," instructed Gaia. "Feel my vast arctic areas which are transmuting due to the melting of my ice caps. Observe how my plants, animals and landed areas are adapting to that change so that you can assist them in their transmutation.

*"Beloved **Northern** Crystal," Gaia spoke into Her crystal, "We are here NOW to free you of the encumbrance of Earth's sorrow and fear and to transmute all your shadow into light and love."*

"Now dear human lightbodies, visualize this Northern Crystal as clear as you see the Violet Flame within its core.

"Look to your right again to remember the unconditional love and stories of ascension that all of you have experienced. Pull these messages into your High Hearth to surround it with unconditional love for ALL life. Now, dear humans, breathe your collective experience of transmutation into the Violet Flame within the crystal."

We were all in such a deep alignment with each other and with Gaia that our personal transmutations became ONE planetary transmutation. As we sent our ascension stories, wrapped in unconditional love into the Northern Crystal, the small Violet Flame burst into a huge fire, transmuting and healing Gaia's **North**.

Instantly, we were transported to the Cornerstone Crystal in the East.

"Please remember your many incarnations in my eastern territories," said Gaia. "Remember the new hope that comes with each sunrise, and the ancient spiritual messages that began in that area, as well as the many incarnations in which you were spiritual guides and masters," Gaia instructed.

*"Beloved **Eastern** Crystal," Gaia decreed, "We are here NOW to free you of the encumbrance of Earth's sorrow and fear and to transmute all your shadow into light and love."*

We sent our ascension stories, wrapped in unconditional love into the Eastern Crystal's small Violet Flame, which burst into a huge fire, transmuting and healing Gaia's **East**.

We were then transported to the Cornerstone Crystal in the South.

"I wish you all to remember your many incarnations in my southern territories. My southern ice caps in the Antarctic are also melting to reveal long kept secrets. See my vast jungles, myriad life forms, huge rivers and ancient societies that live on and are ONE with my land," Gaia instructed.

*"Beloved **Southern** Crystal," Gaia spoke, "We are here NOW to free you of the encumbrance of Earth's sorrow and fear and to transmute all your shadow into light and love."*

We sent our ascension stories, wrapped in unconditional love into the Southern Crystal's small Violet Flame, which burst into a huge fire, transmuting and healing Gaia's **South**.

In a flash, we were standing before the Cornerstone Crystal in the West. Again Gaia proclaimed,

"I wish you all to remember your many incarnations in my western territories. Remember my magnificent sunsets that represent a rest between cycles of change. Embrace the new cycles that are arising from the darkest night into the light of the new day," Gaia instructed.

*"Beloved **Western** Crystal," Gaia called, "We are here NOW to free you of the encumbrance*

of Earth's sorrow and fear and to transmute all your shadow into light and love."

We sent our ascension stories, wrapped in unconditional love into the Western Crystal's small Violet Flame, which burst into a huge fire, transmuting and healing Gaia's **West**.

With the contribution of our personal and collective stories of ascension wrapped with unconditional love, the Violet Flame within each crystal had burst forth in a blaze of glory to transmute all shadow into multidimensional light and love.

We observed as the multidimensional light transmuted the 3D Matrix within each Cornerstone Crystal back into its innate multidimensional matrix. Already we could feel an immense difference in Gaia's Core and wondered how the Earth's topside had changed.

Transmutation of Life Part 5

Transmuting the Core Crystal

JASON SPEAKS:

Before we could further ponder Earth's changes, Gaia transported us all back to the Core Crystal. We felt Mytrian's remembrance of its experience in the Core of Gaia and realized that the "infant Gaia" that Mytrian chased into Earth's core has grown into her maturity.

By re-calibrating the Cornerstone Crystals we had prepared the Core Crystal for the monumental task of re-calibrating Gaia's Earth Matrix back to its true, multidimensional nature. We say "re-calibrating" because Gaia was initially a multidimensional planet.

However, do to the infringement of great darkness on her body, Gaia fell out of the higher grids of Her multidimensional matrix and into the third dimensional grids, with the fourth dimensional matrix being her aura and "dream world."

Just as Gaia's humans have missed the rest of their Multidimensional SELF, Gaia has missed her own higher expressions of SELF. Already, we could feel that Gaia was healing along with Her Nature.

We also felt Her as a mother who was at long last uniting with her lost children. These "lost children" resonated to the higher frequencies beyond Earth's wounded, third dimensional reality. We instinctively know that Gaia's dear sister Venus was supporting Her during her process of "return to SELF."

However, before we could continue our revelations, we were whisked off to the Core Crystal. When we found ourselves before the Core Crystal, it was already clearer and brighter. We were not surprised to see that the Arcturian had a message to share before we transmuted the Core Crystal.

THE ARCTURIAN SPEAKS:
Brave lightbody humans,
We speak to you as the *teachers of the truth* that will be vital when you return topside onto transmuting Earth. We wish to prepare you with a statement that you can share with those who are just awakening to the perceptions of their higher dimensional choices. These choices will be possible because you, our beloved ones, have re-activated the multidimensional light codes of Gaia's Core Crystal.

Please allow the message we will now give you to merge with your Lightbody so that you can repeat when and if you return to

Gaia's transmuting surface. You will tell this message to those who are willing to listen:

"Ages ago Gaia's multidimensional matrix was corrupted with a virus and went 'offline' for many of your incarnations on Earth. With Gaia's multidimensional matrix offline, only the third dimensional perceptions and fourth dimensional dreams were perceptible to your human form. Therefore your persistent memory of your perceptions was limited to third-dimensional patterns of light.

"We want you to know that now Gaia's multidimensional matrix has been totally re-activated. However, many of you have lost all conscious awareness of your Multidimensional SELF who resonates to the higher dimensional grids of Earth's holographic matrix.

"Your many lives of placing your attention on the available third dimensional frequency grids of Earth's holographic matrix amplified the sensations, perceptions and experiences of *only* your physical self.

"Hence, your habitual attachment to the third dimensional grids over-rode your memory that Gaia's matrix was once multidimensional. Because of your persistent perceptual habits, your primary attention was on the third dimensional grids. Eventually, you grew to believe that only the physical world was REAL.

"Because of this small, lower frequency perceptual field, your higher-dimensional Pleiadian and/or Arcturian expressions of SELF who projected their essence into many of your physical earth vessels were invisible to your 3D perceptions.

"We wish to tell you that Gaia's multidimensional matrix has been re-activated. However, the power of habit is very strong. Thus, the first challenge you face will be to remember that YOU are a multidimensional being.

"As you accept that truth, you can 'save' your higher dimensional perceptions and experiences onto Gaia's higher frequency holographic grids. When you save your inter-dimensional experiences on Gaia's newly activated multidimensional matrix, they merge with the multidimensional reality of other earthlings.

"Once your group experience is 'saved' on the Gaia's multidimensional matrix, you can connect with the collective and planetary multidimensional energy field. It is in this manner that inter-dimensional experiences and travel will become *normal.*

"All life on Earth is now connected to Gaia's multidimensional matrix. It is through the shared adventures of this matrix that Gaia's inhabitants are moving beyond the limitations of third dimensional consciousness and into the higher frequencies of Earth's multidimensional reality. At first these higher dimensional activities may be labeled as 'dreams' or 'just your imagination.'

"However, when these dreams and imaginations are communicated to others via the shared grids, they become more ordinary. As the 'new normal' expands, more and more of humanity will feel safe enough to openly share their experiences.

"Fortunately, the animal, plant and elemental kingdoms live in unity consciousness with Gaia and naturally embrace Her return to multidimensionality. Therefore, make sure to ground your higher frequency perceptions and experiences into Gaia's Earth.

"With that grounding, it will be easier for you to remember your inter-dimensional experiences during your daily life. In other words, 'save' your inter-dimensional experiences in both the multidimensional 'hard drive' of the planetary matrix as well as in the 'software' of your physical brain.

"A great disadvantage of the software of your human brain is that it only spans one lifetime and a few dimensions. In order to access all the dimensions and lives of your full SELF, you will need to access the 'hard drive' of Gaia's multidimensional matrix. This matrix is much like a transporter in that it carries the DNA codes of every inhabitant that transports onto Gaia's planet.

"Therefore, through Gaia's 'transporter files,' you will be able to find all the lives in which you have entered Gaia's evolution, your point of origin for that entrance and when you logged in and logged out of that incarnation.

"Most important for your present timeline, you will be able to retrieve the files from all of your incarnations on Earth. In this manner, you can consolidate all that you learned in your many lives on Earth collecting information about planetary ascension.

"Once your consciousness is fully connected to Earth's multidimensional matrix, you will experience the multidimensional light of Gaia's information that constantly flows from Her planetary lightbody into your personal lightbody.

"You may not, yet, be aware of your Lightbody. Nonetheless, it resides within your core ready to burst forth into your daily life.

"To remind yourself of an earthly incarnation in which you lived in total unity and unconditional love, you can 'search' for it on Gaia's multidimensional hard drive to access the light codes for that incarnation.

"Now that Gaia's multidimensional matrix has been re-activated, your transmutation into Lightbody will be greatly facilitated. Hence, conscious information of other incarnation in which you transmuted into Lightbody will be immensely helpful."

We know that all of you who choose to serve on Gaia's surface will be able to carry this message in your heart and lovingly share it with those who are ready.

We, the Arcturians, send you all unconditional love and unconditional thanksgiving for your personal and collective contributions to planetary ascension. We return you now to Gaia who will assist you with the re-calibration process of Her Core Crystal.

JASON CONTINUES:

Gaia returned in her humanoid form to deliver Her message,

"Blessings to all my multidimensional humans," Gaia began. "I am grateful that you have volunteered to assist me in re-calibrating *our* Earth back to the multidimensional expression of my planetary SELF.

"I wish to tell you that because you have participated in re-calibrating the Cornerstone Crystals, when you focus your attention on the Core Crystal you will feel a sense of planetary consciousness that you have never before experienced.

"Therefore, before we transmute the Core Crystal, I ask that you expand your multidimensional consciousness all the way up the frequency trail to your Oversoul SELF."

By now, we were so merged with Gaia, the planet, and each other that our consciousness simultaneously expanded from our fifth dimensional Lightbody, to include our sixth dimensional Light Being and into our seventh dimensional Oversoul.

As we did so, we felt total unity consciousness with each other, with Gaia and with Gaia's Earth.

Since we resonated far beyond the illusion of time, we could easily hold our collective frequency until it was the NOW to align our joined consciousness with Gaia's Core Crystal.

Simultaneously we received an inner message to focus on the Core Crystal to see that a multidimensional matrix was circling up the core of the huge crystal and beyond our vision. We also observed that the third and fourth dimensional grids on the matrix were disconnected from the higher dimensional grids.

It was then that Gaia continued, "My dear multidimensional ones, I ask that each of you first align your consciousness with the third and fourth dimensional grids of my newly awakening multidimensional matrix. I shall send you my unconditional love and thanksgivings as you move into that alignment."

While Gaia patiently waited, we all connected our consciousness with the third and fourth dimensional grids.

As we gradually made that connection, we became more and more unified with Earth. Then, in a burst of light, we were ONE with Gaia's Earth. We were the sky, the ground, the trees, the water, the rain, the animals, plants, insects, fish and the elementals. We all WERE planet Earth.

"Thank you, dear ones," we heard Gaia say from the core of our planetary self. "Now attach your consciousness to the fifth dimensional grids of my multidimensional matrix."

Our response was instant and Gaia's (our) core, surface, sky, water, plants, animals and elementals burst into lightbody. From within our blazing light, we heard Gaia say,

"Beloveds, connect with my sixth dimensional grids *NOW.*"

Within that NOW we were the multidimensional matrix. We were flashes of light that flew across the matrix creating, repairing, recalibrating, and most importantly, unconditionally loving Gaia's multidimensional matrix.

Within the NOW of our sixth dimensional awareness, our light essence created light connections between every first, second, third, fourth, and fifth dimensional life form that was attached to Gaia's multidimensional matrix.

At the edges of our mind, we could experience our myriad planetary lightbodies, auras and physical expressions. We worked as ONE to merge all bodies of light into the Oness of Gaia's multidimensional matrix.

"And NOW beloveds," we heard the distant murmur of Gaia's voice, "welcome your Oversoul to join us."

Suddenly all was silent like the still before a storm, but this was a storm of pure spirit and unconditional love. We felt an immense energy field brewing within our collective planetary self.

We knew better than to fight it and, instead, opened wide the windows of our hearts. In a flash of golden light, the connection was made as the seventh dimensional spirit of our Oversouls merged with the multidimensional matrix of all planetary matter.

"NOW! We will transmute the Core Crystal," we heard Gaia exclaim.

Immediately we had the experience of "Being the Core Crystal." Our Mytrian self shared the juxtaposition for our first visit to the Core Crystal and this great awakening. As we bound the two experiences into a circle of infinity, we heard Gaia say,

*"Beloved **Core** Crystal, you are **NOW** free of **ALL** encumbrance of Earth's sorrow and fear, which is NOW transmuted into multidimensional light and unconditional love! With the full power of your multidimensional matrix re-activated, we open wide our Multidimensional Portal of Ascension."*

With Gaia's statement, the Violet Fire within the Core Crystal, as well as within the core of our personal, planetary and core crystalline hearts burst into a huge Violet Flame of Transmutation. The entire Core of Gaia filled with Violet Light, unconditional love, and the pure joy of ascension.

Our individual Lightbodies had long since merged into a stream of light and love, and we were ONE with each other, ONE with Gaia, and ONE with Multidimensional Earth.

We saw the earth elementals around us glimmer with a violet glow, while the air elementals within Gaia's core cast the aroma of a million violets on a spring morning. The fire elementals transmuted from red to violet and the water elementals danced upon the violet ripples of light.

Gaia's core became hotter and hotter until we feared that something would burst. But, instead of bursting, something opened. Just above the Core Crystal a huge portal emerged.

Through the slowly opening portal we could see that all the grids of Gaia's 3D Matrix had reconnected with the long lost fourth, fifth, sixth and seventh dimensional grids of the reconnected multidimensional matrix. We could also see even higher dimensional grids of the matrix, which were ready to be joined and activated.

As we looked into the portal to see the myriad versions of New Earth, we cried, laughed, sang and stood in reverent silence. Finally, we all settled into reverent silence, unconditional love and eternal thanksgiving.

Through The Portal

As if in response to our unasked question of, "What do we do now?" Gaia said, "My beloved ones, as you rejoice around the Core Crystal, I ask that you return to my surface to gather groups who will repeat this ceremony again and again.

"You, my beloved volunteers, have taken a form to assist me during the NOW of my planetary transmutation. However, there is the constant threat of darkness on the surface of my third dimensional body. Thus, just as you must continually clean your physical house, you will need to continually repeat this ceremony on my physical planet.

"With the recalibration of my Cornerstone and Core Crystals, I will be able to maintain an opened multidimensional portal into the higher dimensions of my planetary self. Some of you will travel through this portal to populate fifth dimensional New Earth.

"Some of you will return to your higher dimensional starships, and some of you will maintain your current physical, earth vessel to continue your support of my planetary ascension. Whatever you choose, I deeply thank all of you for your boundless service.

"For those of you who wish to remain with my planetary adventure, I will see you on whatever frequency of multidimensional New Earth that you choose."

With Gaia's final words, the huge portal opened wide into Gaia's higher dimensional worlds. We all stood in awe as we looked up into the portal to see myriad choices of higher dimensional expressions of Gaia.

"There are so many possible realities," I whispered to Sandy who was within and next to me, "Which one do you choose?"

"I choose the reality in which we are *always* together," said Sandy as she put her arm through mine.

Through The Portal

I close this book with the very first message I received:

April 11, 2012

TRANSMISSIONS FROM HOME

After a long dream of being in someone else's house and realizing it was time for me to leave and go to my own house, I woke up at 5:55 with the words, "Transmissions from Home."

When I heard the words, "transmissions from Home," I saw a man sitting at a desk, like a newscaster. He was blond and had on a uniform, which looked similar to the uniform of a Galactic Being. His uniform was white and gold with an insignia over his heart.

There were also golden adornments on his shoulders and his collar was straight up, as with a military uniform. In fact, it seemed to be a Dress Military Uniform, but not from our military.

I got up and went into my office to get my transmission. I turned on the computer and wrote, "I am ready for your transmission now. Would you please send me your message?" My answer was,

"Dearest Members of Earth,

Suzanne Lie, Ph.D.

"We are members of the Galactic Federation speaking to you today to tell you that our landings have begun. We come first to our awakened ones within their dreams and meditations. We are here to speak to all who can receive our messages so that we can prepare you. Then, you can prepare others."

From that first message, the Pleiadians story rushed through my fingers. Most of the time, I felt as though I was reading for the first time as I wrote it. I share the story as I received it in the hope that it touches your heart and changes your life as much as it did mine.

See you in the higher dimensions,

Suzanne Lie

About the Author

Suzanne Lie Ph.D.

Suzanne Lie, Ph.D., has been a seeker since she was a child where her active "imagination" took her deep into her inner life. Suzanne first stepped onto her spiritual path in the mid-1970s when she met her first spiritual teacher. Since then, she has had many teachers and initiations.

Her life in the physical plane was quite "normal" as her spiritual work provided her with the confidence to continue her educational training to obtain a Ph.D. in Clinical Psychology. Her studies included

Suzanne Lie, Ph.D.

personal psychotherapy and focused on alternative methods of psychotherapy, such as hypnotherapy and guided meditation, which gave her tools to help herself, as well as others.

In 1999, after two years of prompting from the Arcturians, she began sharing her insights on her website, www.multidimensions.com, where her full spiritual journey is described. "Coming out" of the spiritual closet was not easy, but fortunately, documenting her journey and talking to others all over the world with similar experiences allowed her to fully accept and embrace her true SELF.

Once she built a solid foundation of knowledge regarding the journey back to the multidimensional SELF, she began writing the two volumes of the book, ***Becoming ONE, People and Planet: A Manual for Personal and Planetary Transformation.***

She continues to regularly share her experiences and Arcturian teachings on her blog, ***Awakening with Suzanne Lie,*** and she wishes to help awakening ones come out of hiding and allow the glory of their highest expression of SELF into their everyday life.

Through The Portal

Explorations into the incarnation and connection of twin flames and divine complements are detailed in her book, ***Visions from Venus***, and her book ***Reconstructing Reality*** describes the process of awakening to past or *parallel* lives and incarnations.

She is excited to share her latest 5-book series, ***Pleiadian Perspective on Ascension***, which details the entire process of an ascending planet designed to assist humanity with its current transition into a higher dimension.

Recognizing the need for comprehensive educational training and guidance in multidimensionality, she has recently developed **Multidimensional Leadership Training** programs, in conjunction with the Arcturians, designed to train new leaders that will bring forth expanded, synchronistic guidance, support, leadership, and governance in the societal shift.

All of her initiatives remind us that through seeking, communicating with, and integrating our true, multidimensional SELF into our physical life, we can greatly expand our consciousness and regain latent skills that will assist us in creating our new reality.

Suzanne Lie, Ph.D.

Suzanne is available for personal sessions and would love to connect with and assist those ready to explore multidimensionality and who feel drawn to the Arcturian teachings.

<u>www.multidimensions.com</u>

Through The Portal

Other Books by the Author
www.multidimensions.com

The Journal — When Ordinary People Get Extraordinary Information
When Lisa finally arrived at her childhood home, her mother was gone. All that greeted her was her mother's journal, which she decided to read.

A New Home — Pleiadian Perspective on Ascension Book 1
How it All Began — It's April eleventh 2012, and the California sun was still below the horizon. After a long complex dream of being in someone else's house, I realized it was time for me to leave. I got up and went into my office to receive this transmission. I am ready for your transmission now.

Life on the Mothership — Pleiadian Perspective on Ascension Book 2
There were just the two of us in the ship. I had not been on the Ship very long when I had my first experience of the Mothership's Oversoul. I had been there long enough, however, to understand that the ship was a living, multidimensional being.

Suzanne Lie, Ph.D.

The Landing Party — Pleiadian Perspective on Ascension Book 3
Mytre and Mytria have "landed" within the consciousness of earthbound Jason and Sandy and are in the process of assisting them to awaken to their Higher Self. Jason and Sandy meet each other, fall in love and totally alter their lives to encompass their greater purpose, which includes unlocking the mystery of their multidimensional reality.

It Is the NOW — Pleiadian Perspective on Ascension Book 4
Featuring a possible reality in which both humans and Pleiadians, with the help of Mytrian and the Arcturian, could serve in unity to transcend a planet. It Is The NOW is a "science fiction" that presents a possible reality of "scientific fact." Join us on our inter-galactic and inter-dimensional travels that bring us back to creating a new home.

Through the Portal — Pleiadian Perspective on Ascension Book 5
Big changes are about to occur on planet Earth, and leadership training is needed for Sandy and Jason. But when they return to Earth, that which they thought they would change, changed them instead. Follow this amazing "final act" that is actually a new beginning.

Through The Portal

Becoming ONE, People and Planet: A Manual for Personal and Planetary Transformation Volume One
This series is a masterful blend of psychology, metaphysics, ecology, science, art, and spirituality. This book offers information, meditations, and exercises…

Becoming One, Becoming ONE, People and Planet: A Manual for Personal and Planetary Transformation Volume Two
This series is a masterful blend of psychology, metaphysics, ecology, science, art, and spirituality. This book offers more information, meditations, and exercises…

Visions from Venus, A Multidimensional Love Story, Book 1
This journey begins with Shature's descent into the third dimension, then to a new home in the fourth dimension, and ends with her return to the third dimension in search of her other half. Fact and fantasy intertwine…

Reconstructing Reality, Book 2 of Visions from Venus
Most of us do not remember that we have volunteered to remember our multidimensional heritage and unite with our true SELF in the higher worlds. Remembering this unity would be difficult indeed with the knowledge of only one lifetime…

Suzanne Lie, Ph.D.

Thirty Veils Of Illusion
When Illusion is removed, all that remains is Truth. This book should really be entitled, "My Thirty Veils of Illusion," as I'm sure that each person who journeys inside himself or herself would find their own thirty illusions, or more…

Journey Through the Arcturian Corridor — Part I
The Arcturian Corridor is a tunnel of light, which serves as an inter-dimensional portal between the physical realms and the higher worlds of the fifth dimension and beyond…

The Journey Continues: Arcturian Corridor — Part II

The Journey Continues: Arcturian Corridor — Part III

Preparing for the Return: Arcturian Corridor — Part IV

Seven Steps to Soul: A Poetic Journey of Spiritual Awakening
Seven Steps to Soul is a poetic and therapeutic journey of spiritual awakening. The seven sections of this book represent seven processes that align us with our Soul…

Through The Portal

What Did You Learn?

Welcome to the Land of Inner Peace and Limitless Joy. Have you learned the secrets of creating the reality YOU desire? For, indeed, life is YOUR creation. As the illusions of our physical reality end, and we return to…

The Violet Temple

Join us as we calibrate our consciousness to activate our personal Merkaba, so that we can take a Journey to the Central Sun, Alycone, The Pleiades. Once there we will meet Mytria, who will guide us through the Violet Temple…

A Child's Adventure In Faerie – For The Child Within Us All

Most of us do not turn within to ask for answers until we are forced to do so by feelings of failure or experiences of fear and pain in our outer world. Our inner life may hold pain and sorrow…

More books on their way, so please stay tuned to **www.multidimensions.com**

Made in the USA
Middletown, DE
24 September 2017